The
Pentagon
Propaganda
Machine

SENATOR J. W. FULBRIGHT

The
Pentagon
Propaganda
Machine

LIVERIGHT NEW YORK

355.0335
F95p
74195
April, 1971

1.987654321

Standard Book Number: 87140-522-9
Library of Congress Catalog Card Number: 79-131268

Designed by Charlotte Thorp

Manufactured in the United States of America

Contents

Acknowledgments

This book represents an expansion of a series of speeches given on the Senate floor in December of 1969. My aim at that time, as it is now, was to make the Senate and the public at large aware of the multi-faceted and quietly pervasive nature of the Defense Department's public relations activity. In effect, then, this book should be regarded as an instructional manual.

It would take an additional volume, and someone more schooled than I in the communications/public opinion field to study the impact these Defense Department activities have had on our thinking as a nation.

I am indebted to Edward A. O'Neill for his assistance in the preparation of this book and to the officials, officers, and men of the Department of Defense and the separate services who—in response to my questions—supplied the raw information which provides the foundation for this book.

Senator J. W. Fulbright

The
Pentagon
Propaganda
Machine

1 | The Starbird Memorandum

IN SEPTEMBER, 1968, Secretary of the Army Stanley R. Resor sent to the then Secretary of Defense Clark M. Clifford two "classified" memoranda. One was Resor's own; the other, a detailed, fifteen-page document, had been put together by Lieutenant General Alfred D. Starbird, "manager" of the Sentinel System, the Johnson Administration's version of the ABM. Together the papers spelled out a coordinated high-pressure propaganda and public relations program, to be undertaken by various branches of the armed forces, designed to sell the ABM to the American public.

At the time, the Johnson Administration was running into trouble with its proposal to deploy fifteen to twenty missile sites around the country to protect major American cities against possible Communist Chinese attack. Pentagon officials were getting worried about public reaction. Army Secretary Resor's memorandum reflected that concern, saying there was "public confusion" about the need for such a missile defense system. "I feel it essential," he wrote, "that the Army undertake a time-phased public affairs program to provide information to dispel this public confusion."

General Starbird noted that there was opposition to ABM "in certain segments of Congress, in scientific circles, and in citizen-public official interest groups." His list of reasons for congressional and scientific opposition—reasons as valid today as they were then—included "technical and operational feasibility, cost, disarmament, the international arms race, and national priorities." He was less exact in describing the reasons for community opposition, but what he said acknowledged the understandable displeasure a large number of citizens were voicing over having nuclear warheads virtually in their backyards.

Although designed initially to persuade the public that billions of dollars should be spent on a particular weapon, its long-term aim was to intervene in the decision-making process at the congressional level where complex questions of foreign and domestic priorities compete in an area outside the competence of the military. General Starbird's memorandum recognized that the basic wisdom of the ABM proposal was doubted by many honest and technically competent people. Nearly a year after the Army set up the Sentinel publicity program, forty-nine members of the Senate expressed that doubt when they voted against Safeguard, the Nixon Administration's diluted version of the Sentinel System.

In size and intensity, the Sentinel publicity program rivaled anything the military had tried in recent years in support of one specific weapons program. Since the battle over unification in the late 1940s when the services vigor-

2

ously competed for status there have been a series of similar efforts. Each impinged on the traditional system for making general public policy. The ABM campaign, for example, directly affected the national welfare and national interests, and security. Its details were kept secret from the public and parts of its operation were so designed that the Army's hand would not be visible even after the campaign was in full swing.

Five months passed from the time the Resor and Starbird memoranda went to Secretary Clifford before their existence became known to the public. Even then, the information did not come from the Pentagon but from a newspaper, the *Washington Post*. On February 16, 1969, the *Post* carried a front-page story by Philip Geyelin about the memoranda, saying high Army officials were conducting "an extraordinarily intricate and comprehensive campaign" to persuade the American people and their representatives in the Congress of the need for the ABM. The newspaper, in an editorial the following day, labeled the campaign "The Big ABM Brainwash."

There were indeed many elements of "brainwashing" in the campaign. Congressional and scientific criticism had been voiced and opposition developed in the two cities first selected as Sentinel sites.

In September 1968, however, a true national discussion of the desirability of the ABM deployment and the far-reaching implications of that decision had not fully developed. The public as a whole was relatively uninformed. The Pentagon timing, from a public relations man's point of view, was good. But its aim—to manipulate public opinion using all the weapons in the Pentagon PR arsenal, so that

3

ultimately Congress might be influenced in a matter of such importance—was not good.

Such treatment of the legislative branch is not new—as our involvements in Vietnam, Laos and Cambodia testify Since the 1950s, as we have moved from crisis to crisis, the constitutional responsibilities of the Congress have been eroded in dangerous measure by the diversion of power to the President and the Joint Chiefs and the Department of State.

Under circumstances of continuing threat to national security, it is hardly surprising that the military should have become an active, and powerful, participant in the policy-making process. Bringing to bear a discipline, unanimity, and strength of conviction seldom found among civilian officials, the able and energetic men who fill the top ranks of the armed services have acquired an influence dispropor-tionate to their numbers on our national policy. It is under-standable, therefore, that the Army should have organized and vigorously conducted the campaign for the Sentinel System. Nonetheless, it is wrong—and after I had obtained copies of the Resor and Starbird memoranda from the Army I found out how wrong.

Resor's memorandum outlined the kinds of activities the Army would pursue. There would be more news releases and pictures of the Sprint and Spartan missiles to be used in the system and of hitherto unpublicized firings of these missiles at the Kwajalein Missile Range in the South Pacific. Film clips would be distributed to television stations. Edi-tors, reporters, and broadcasters would be taken to Kwaja-lein and to the White Sands Missile Range in New Mexico to watch missile firings. "Information kits" would be distributed for use in countering criticism. A complex and expensive model of a Sentinel installation would be built and taken on a tour of the communities chosen as missile sites. Army speakers would be sent to speak to civic, patriotic, and technical groups. Sentinel representatives also would visit local editors, publishers, and broadcasters to explain the ABM system to them. Similar visits would be made to senior state, city, and county officials. And the Army would "take the initiative" to see that all Senators and Representatives "from affected areas" would be given classified briefings, similar to those already given to members of Congress from the Boston and Seattle areas where there had been public complaints after the announcement of the establishment of ABM sites near those two cities.

A particularly disturbing part of Resor's memorandum was a proposal to recruit scientists to support the ABM. "Several highly placed and reputable U.S. scientists," he wrote, "have spoken out in print against the Sentinel missile system." He named a few of them—Hans Bethe, George Kistiakowsky, and Jerome Weisner, the latter two former Science Advisers to Presidents Eisenhower and Kennedy. Resor's list could have been longer, for all of the men who served as Science Advisors to President Kennedy and President Johnson were critical of the feasibility of the ABM, as were several who had been chiefs of the Department of Defense's research and development branch.

Resor went on to say:

It is essential that all possible questions raised by these opponents be answered, preferably by nongovernmental scientists.

We will be in contact shortly with scientists who are familiar with the Sentinel program and who may see fit to write articles

5

for publication supporting the technical feasibility and operational effectiveness of the Sentinel System.

We shall extend to these scientists all practical assistance.

The *Washington Post* editorially observed, "What are we to make of the next learned dissertation published by a scientist? Will it be his handiwork or General Starbird's?"

To my knowledge, no procured articles were published. Even if they were not, the possibility that such articles might have been written on order and "with all practical assistance" from the Department of the Army to promote a weapons system is a perversion of the scientific method.

Most of the Starbird Memorandum was concerned with spelling out details in support of Resor's project and with establishing the "time phase" through which the program would proceed. However, it too contained some disturbing ideas. For example, "Personnel affiliated with the Sentinel Public Affairs Program* will cooperate with industry on public relation efforts by industries involved in the Sentinel Program." Such cooperation presumably could be easily obtained, and would add to the propaganda arsenal of the Army the huge public relations facilities of billion-dollar corporations whose profits came from military contracts. Richard Rovere wrote in the *New Yorker* about this part of the program, "The military . . . has more money than anyone else, and when its vast funds are added to those of the industries it deals with, it seems to have about all the money there is." The hand of the Army would, of course, not be visible in industry's advertising the need for ABM,

---

* This group included representatives of the Army's Chief of Information, Chief of Legislative Liaison, Chief of Engineers, Chief of Research and Development, and the Deputy Chief of Staff, Operations.

6

just as it would not have been visible in the learned and favorable articles done by civilian scientists.

General Starbird also directed that an already existing Army program known as "Operation Understanding" should be adapted for promotion of the Sentinel. "Operation Understanding" had been used for a number of years to fly "civic leaders" in Army aircraft to facilities such as the North American Air Defense Command's underground center and headquarters at Colorado Springs, Colorado, for "orientation." The purpose of this "orientation" was obvious, as an Army report from pre-Sentinel days shows: "One group from Ohio reported after their tour that 'Operation Understanding' was very educational and thought provoking. . . . We entreat the support of the Congress of the United States on behalf of the U.S. Army Air Defense."

General Starbird's approach was that the Corps of Engineers' offices around the country should select "citizen leaders from local communities adjacent to potential Sentinel sites" to be given the "Operation Understanding" treatment. The White Sands Missile Range in New Mexico, one of the two places Secretary Resor proposed that newsmen be taken, replaced Colorado Springs on the tour's itinerary. During 1968 the Army took 618 persons there, at least two-thirds of whom, an examination of Army community relations reports showed, were from areas announced as potential Sentinel sites.

A representative group which made the Fort Bliss–White Sands–Colorado Springs tour was twenty-seven women from northern and central New Jersey. With their military escort of eight local National Guard officers—including a major general and his aide—they were picked up at Trenton,

January 30, 1969, by an Air Force C-141 transport plane and brought home three days later.

"We had an excellent time," one of the women recalled recently, "and it was very educational. I don't mean that the way it sounds; what I mean is that there was a very positive cast to all of the things we saw and were told."

She said the group went first to Fort Bliss, where they toured the headquarters, were shown models of several types of missiles and lectured on their roles in air defense, and were given a briefing by the commanding general, who later was their host at a cocktail party.

"This was just about the time that there were protests in Boston about placing Sentinel missiles there, and several of the women asked about them. The impression I got from the answers was 'Now, don't worry. You're in good hands with the Army taking care of things.' "

The following day, the group was taken seventy miles by bus to the White Sands Test Area to see scheduled missile firings.

"They fired four missiles I think at drone planes, but they were too high to see though we could see the bursts," the woman said. "One of the missiles went crazily off course and they had to 'destruct' it, they told us. That part wasn't very reassuring."

From Fort Bliss, the group was taken to NORAD headquarters at Colorado Springs for more briefings at that impressive, underground facility ("I would have liked to have seen what was behind all those closed doors" our visitor said), and then back to Trenton.

"I think all of us were very impressed by all we saw,"

the woman said. "The whole thing ran like clockwork. I must say the Army is good at scheduling."

Although it is unlikely that all the visitors who went to White Sands reacted as enthusiastically as the Ohio group, who entreated the Congress to support air defense, many undoubtedly succumbed to the VIP treatment they received. The military is most adept at this treatment, and when it adds breathtaking demonstrations of missile firings and intensely singleminded briefings, it is small wonder that it can overcome the doubts of the unwary.

A few days after the Resor–Starbird story broke, Secretary of Defense Melvin R. Laird was asked at a press conference if the Pentagon was engaged in a "propaganda" campaign to push the Sentinel System. Secretary Laird strongly denied that it was. Despite the Secretary's disclaimer, the records disclose that in February 1969, the Army was conducting a campaign inherited from the previous Administration that can only be described as "propaganda."

The word "propaganda" in current usage implies some degree of subterfuge. And there certainly was subterfuge involved in the Army's promotion campaign for Sentinel. The attempt to get scientists to support the program and the alliance with military contractors, along with other elements of the project, had been hidden from public view. Though the Resor and Starbird memoranda were not classified documents in the strict security sense, they were labeled "For Official Use Only." This label is stamped on papers to keep them privy to the bureaucracy, and once the label is affixed the chances of anyone outside seeing them

9

—unless they are specifically asked for—are nil. Such papers are said to be "administratively controlled."

A few weeks after the press conference at which he was questioned about Sentinel propaganda, Secretary Laird sent a memorandum—unclassified—to the top command, civilian and military, of his department. In it he said:

I intend that the Department of Defense shall conduct all of its activities in an open manner, consistent with the need for security. . . . No information will be classified solely because disclosure might result in criticism of the Department of Defense. . . . Our obligation to provide the public with accurate, timely information on major Department of Defense programs will require in some instances detailed public information planning and coordination within the Department and with other government agencies. However, I want to emphasize that the sole purpose of such planing and coordination will be to expedite the flow of information to the public. *Propaganda has no place in the Department of Defense public information programs.* [Italics are Secretary Laird's.]

At about the same time that he issued these instructions, Secretary Laird told Representative John E. Moss of California, chairman of the House Subcommittee on Government Information, that he was opposed to the Sentinel public relations program and that it would not be carried out. However, "Operation Understanding" tours of White Sands are still going on, and representatives of the North American Air Defense Command are still traveling the country making speeches for Safeguard, President Nixon's version of the ABM. The other aspects of the promotion campaign seem to have been abandoned by the Administration, although the ABM matter is still very much alive.

Even after Secretary Laird's "no propaganda" order, the

implications of the Pentagon's campaign to sell ABM continued to trouble me. It is one thing for the military to advise the Executive and the Congress on matters involving national defense. That is a part of its job. It is quite another to mount a concerted nation-wide propaganda and public relations campaign seeking public and congressional support for a program of arguable effectiveness and validity. If the military had the potential to organize a campaign of the scope and complexity set forth in the Starbird Memorandum, what other kinds of public relations programs did it have and how far-ranging were they? To get the answers, my staff drew up sets of detailed questions about Defense Department public relations activities and sent them to the Pentagon and the three armed services.

The results of these inquiries amazed me for I had had no idea of the extent to which the Pentagon had been staffed and armed to promote itself and the military services. In use is every device and technique of the commercial public relations man and even some that he cannot afford such as cruises on aircraft carriers and "firepower" demonstrations by battalions of artillery and squadrons of aircraft, all designed to shape public opinion and build an impression that militarism is good for you.

A most unsettling aspect of these various campaigns was the scant attention the disclosure of their existence attracted and the lack of reaction from the American people who were being sold a bill of goods. This complaisant acceptance of things military is one of the most ominous developments in modern America.

It seems to me that we have grown distressingly used to war. For more than fourteen of the past twenty-eight years

11

we have been fighting somewhere, and we have been ready to fight almost anywhere for the other fourteen. War and the military have become a part of our environment, like pollution.

Violence is our most important product. We have been spending nearly $80 billion a year on the military, which is more than the profits of all American business, or, to make another comparison, is almost as much as the total spending of the federal, state, and local governments for health, education, old age and retirement benefits, housing, and agriculture. Until the past session of the Congress, these billions have been provided to the military with virtually no questions asked.

The military has been operating for years in that Elysium of the public relations man, a seller's market. Take the climate into which the Sentinel ABM program was introduced. Many people looked on it, as they now look on Safeguard, not as a weapon but as a means of prosperity. For the industrialist it meant profits; for the worker new jobs and the prospect of higher wages; for the politician a new installation or defense order with which to ingratiate himself with his constituents. Military expenditures today provide the livelihood of some ten percent of our work force. There are 22,000 major corporate defense contractors and another 100,000 subcontractors. Defense plants or installations are located in 363 of the country's 435 congressional districts. Even before it turns its attention to the public-at-large, the military has a large and sympathetic audience for its message.

These millions of Americans who have a vested interest

in the expensive weapons systems spawned by our global military involvements are as much a part of the military-industrial complex as the generals and the corporation heads. In turn they have become a powerful force for the perpetuation of those involvements, and have had an indirect influence on a weapons development policy that has driven the United States into a spiraling arms race with the Soviet Union and made us the world's major salesman of armaments.

A Marine war hero and former Commandant of the Corps, General David M. Shoup, has said, "America has become a militaristic and aggressive nation." He could be right. Militarism has been creeping up on us during the past thirty years. Prior to World War II, we never maintained more than a token peacetime army. Even in 1940, with Nazi Germany sweeping over Europe, there were fewer than half a million men in all of the armed services. The Army, which then included the Air Corps, had one general and four lieutenant generals. In October 1941, six weeks before Pearl Harbor, the extension of the draft law was passed by but a single vote. Many of those who voted no did so for partisan political reasons, but antimilitarism certainly was a consideration for some. Today we have more than 3.5 million men in uniform and nearly 28 million veterans of the armed forces in the civilian population. The Air Force alone has twelve four-star generals and forty-two lieutenant generals. The American public has become so conditioned by crises, by warnings, by words that there are few, other than the young, who protest against what is happening.

The situation is such that last year Senator Allen J. Ellender of Louisiana, hardly an apostle of the New Left, felt constrained to say:

"For almost twenty years now, many of us in the Congress have more or less blindly followed our military spokesmen. Some have become captives of the military. We are on the verge of turning into a military nation."

This militarism that has crept up on us is bringing about profound changes in the character of our society and government—changes that are slowly undermining democratic procedure and values.

Confronted in the past generation with a series of challenges from dynamic totalitarian powers, we have felt ourselves compelled to imitate some of the methods of our adversaries. I do not share the view that American fears of Soviet and Chinese aggressiveness have been universally paranoiac, although I think there have been a fair number of neurotic anxieties expressed. The point is that the very objective we pursue—the preservation of a free society—proscribes certain kinds of policies even though they might be tactically expedient. We cannot, without doing ourselves the very injury that we seek to secure ourselves against from foreign adversaries, pursue policies which rely primarily on the threat or use of force, because policies of force and the pre-eminence given to the wielders of force—the military—are inevitably disruptive of democratic values. Alexis de Tocqueville, that wisest of observers of American democracy, put it this way:

War does not always give democratic societies over to military government, but it must invariably and immeasurably increase the powers of civil government; it must almost automatically concentrate the direction of all men and the control of all things in the hands of the government. If that does not lead to despotism by sudden violence, it leads men gently in that direction by their habits.*

During the twenty years Senator Ellender cited we have not only been infected by militarism but by another virus as virulent—an ideological obsession about communism. The head of steam built up in the country by the late Joe McCarthy has never really been blown off, and the extremists of the right utilize it to keep the hatreds that have developed over the years as hot as possible. This heat and the ideas espoused by these extremists produce such deceptively quick and simple solutions as "Bomb Hanoi!" Or "Overthrow Castro!" Or "America: Love It or Leave It!" If we would only proclaim and pursue our dedication to total victory over world communism, they say, root out the subversives—real and imaginary—at home, make our allies follow our lead in world affairs, all of our troubles would soon be solved.

This heated climate makes militarism luxuriate, for the military solution is also the simple solution. I am not, of course, implying that the men of our military forces are of the extreme right. They are in the main patriotic, hard-working, worried men, but their parochial talents have been given too much scope in our topsy-turvy world. There is little in the education, training, or experience of most soldiers to equip them with the balance of judgment needed to play the political role they they now hold in our society.

* Alexis de Tocqueville, *Democracy in America,* vol. 2 (New York: Harper & Row, 1965), p. 625.

15

The nation needs its military men as brave and dedicated public servants. We can get along without them as mentors and opinion-molders. These roles have never been and, in a time when subtlety of mind and meticulous attention to questions of right over might ought to command us, should not now be their proper business.

2 | Information to Propaganda

IN 1967, THE ASSOCIATED PRESS estimated that the Executive branch of the Federal Government was spending $400 million a year on public information and public relations. That was about $70 million above the amount spent the same year on the Congress and the Federal judiciary. Perhaps an even more telling comparison was made by William Rivers and Wilbur Schramm in their book *Responsibility in Mass Communication*:

All together, federal expenditures on telling and showing the taxpayers are more than double the combined costs of newsgathering by the two major U.S. wire services, the three major television networks, and the ten largest American newspapers.*

Of course not all of the estimated $400 million was being spent on publicity, news releases, and special pleadings. The Federal Government has a responsibility for providing the

* New York: Harper & Row, Publishers, 1969, p. 97.

general public with that information which it alone has the resources to compile. Such information ranges from the daily weather forecast to the monthly Consumer Price Index to the decennial census. The influence of this information on daily living, public attitudes, economic developments, and political decisions is as wide-ranging as the subjects themselves.

Although a Weather Bureau forecast of rain may only bring out umbrellas and raincoats, a hurricane warning can mobilize the resources of an entire region. A Coast and Geodetic Survey chart of the Chesapeake Bay may keep a weekend sailor from running aground, but it also guides a laden tanker to port. The Agricultural Research Service's booklet *Removing Stains from Fabrics* may be a housewife's boon, but the Department of Agriculture's crop report can influence the whole farm economy. The price index compiled and published by the Bureau of Labor Statistics affects the wage rates of millions of workers and national economic policy as well. A shift in population found through the census can change a state's representation in the Congress.

In 1967, the year the Associated Press made its estimate of federal public relations expenditures, the Library of Congress published a 411-page book that lists the information resources of the Federal Government. The subject index, which ranges from "Acceleration effects" to "Zooplankton," alone runs to 100 pages. Despite the number and diversity of all of these government fact-gathering agencies, the demands made on them by the public are simple: The information they provide must be factual; it must be timely, and it must be available.

Over the years, with very rare exceptions, the information provided to the public through the Federal Government's departments and agencies has been as accurate as the limits of statistical dependability and human error allow. By and large, the information is kept as up to date as current knowledge and analysis can make it. And the information is made available in massive amounts through the communications media, through free distribution, and by sale.

The Government Printing Office receipts from sales to the general public in Fiscal Year 1969 amounted to $19,-907,291. All but a very small part of this was paid for material of a purely informational nature. The demand for speeches by the President, policy statements by Cabinet officers, and transcripts of congressional hearings, all produced by the printing office, is small, but booklets like the Internal Revenue Service's *Sales and Other Dispositions of Depreciable Property* sell by the hundreds of thousands. Free distribution also is large. For example, more than 13 million copies of the Department of Agriculture's *Home and Garden Bulletin* are distributed each year by the Federal Extension Service, by members of Congress, or to persons who have requested the publication. There are many other specialized publications that are sold. Five times a week the Department of Commerce publishes *Commerce Business Daily,* which lists government contracts open for bidding and other material. Nation-wide progress in educational research is made available country-wide through *Research in Education* published by the Department of Health, Education, and Welfare. Harbor conditions and navigation advice are included in the Coast Guard's *Weekly Notices to Mar-*

19

iners. Scores of similar publications regularly issue news, statistics, advice, and instructions on which citizens can depend.

The assembly and dissemination of such information by the Federal Government cannot be faulted except by the most captious of critics. However, when the government moves from pure information to propaganda a border is crossed. Here, nice distinctions arise.

In our governmental system, the need for an informed electorate is more than a copybook maxim. The power of our leaders stems from the people, who must know what their leaders are doing, what they intend to do, and what problems they face. The President must seek public approval of the programs he wants to carry out, and his Cabinet and the other officers appointed by him must strive to make the programs for which they are responsible understood and accepted. To fill this public and executive need successive Administrations have built a public relations apparatus that is now of staggering size.

It is unlikely that anyone in the Federal Government knows how many people are engaged in "opinion-shaping" information activities. It is hard to separate the man who, let us say, is writing a technical paper on irrigation from the man who is writing a speech for his Assistant Secretary intended to sell a controversial policy, especially since the same man may very well do both jobs on successive days. According to columnist James J. Kilpatrick, the late Senator Harry F. Byrd, at the time the Department of Agriculture was promoting the Brannan Plan in 1951, delved into federal public relations activities and "positively identified" 4,200 persons who were so engaged. The Senator, Kilpatrick said, suspected that "double or triple" that number were in fact involved.*

There have been numerous attempts to curb the activities and limit the size of the government's public relations apparatus. Senator Byrd found such efforts reported in the *Congressional Record* as early as 1913. Successes were few and brief, as will be noted in later pages. Congress's only fully successful effort was the curb put on the United States Information Agency when it was formed in 1953. This agency, which is the government's overseas propaganda arm, produces newspapers, magazines, films, television and radio programs, some of excellent quality and some conceivably suitable for domestic distribution. But the Congress, recognizing that a propaganda agency should not propagandize the taxpayers who are paying for the program, forbade USIA to distribute its material in the United States. (Exceptions to this limitation were made for two films, one of the then Mrs. Jacqueline Kennedy's visit to India and Pakistan in 1962 and the other, *Years of Lightning, Day of Drums,* concerning the career and funeral of the late President John F. Kennedy.)

So long as the public relations efforts of the Executive branch are fairly and honestly conducted, criticism of them can scarcely go beyond that arising from careful surveillance of the enormous cost of the apparatus to the taxpayers. Given the nature of modern life and the complexity of our country, this apparatus, built not only to inform but to shape public opinion, is not of itself a bad thing. But what is one to think when the apparatus is used, as we all know it sometimes is, to guide public opinion toward controversial ob-

* *Evening Star,* Washington, D.C., Dec. 9, 1969.

jectives? What of the use of the government's information resources to promote intensely controversial political or foreign policy objectives?

During the past several years, there have been too many instances of lack of candor and of outright misleading statements in treating with the public. Too often we have been misled by the very apparatus that is supposed to keep us factually informed or, in the very strictest sense, honestly guided.

Even without breaking the limits of honest presentation, any President and the heads of his "newsmaking" departments can shape the flow of information the public gets. The President has ready access to the nation's television networks whenever he feels the need to use them, and his press conferences attract hundreds of newsmen. His statements and the statements of the Secretary of State and the Secretary of Defense usually get front page treatment. Through selectivity and timing, they can command attention that at times is far greater than that deserved by the content of the information released. They can give new luster to old ideas and obliterate embarrassing events with announcements, actions, trips, and "summit meetings." In a pinch, what have been called "pseudoevents" can be created. The Executive branch's dominance of "opinion-molding" calls to mind an observation of Judge Learned Hand's that is not inapposite here although it concerned freedom of the press. In his decision upholding the government's monopoly case against the Associated Press some years ago, Judge Hand wrote:

"The First Amendment presupposes that right conclusions are more likely to be gathered out of a multitude of tongues than through any authoritative selection. To many this is, and always will be, folly; but we have staked upon it our all."

Nevertheless, with the responsibility of running the government, the top level of the Executive branch perforce must restrict its efforts at persuasion to the broadest aspects of policies and programs. The day-by-day, drop-by-drop process of opinion-molding is in the hands of the thousands of people in the information apparatus. The workings of these lower level opinion-molders would seem to be unexceptionable. Practically all of the agencies of the Federal Government are open to full public scrutiny. Their information officers are usually helpful; their officials open to inquiry. The Freedom of Information Act makes it mandatory that virtually everything the government does is "unclassified." But the massiveness of the bureaucracy makes it difficult for even the most enterprising of Washington reporters always to get the information that would truly inform his readers. As a result, much of the news of government activity reaches the public from press releases.

There are parts of the Executive branch, however, which can block inquiry on grounds of "security." There can be no argument in today's chaotic and dangerous world of the need for security regulations, so long as they are honestly applied. But the definition of "security" can frequently be an arbitrary and capricious one. On January 17, 1966, a B-52 bomber carrying four hydrogen bombs collided over Palomares, Spain, with a tanker-aircraft. The two planes crashed, and the bombs were strewn over the area. One was lost in the Mediterranean Sea. For forty-four days there was no official acknowledgement by the U.S. Government

23

that hydrogen bombs were involved, although the story was pieced together from various sources and published throughout the world. No acknowledgement was made because Spain wanted no announcement.

In his book, *Confirm or Deny,* Phil G. Goulding, a former Assistant Secretary of Defense for Public Affairs, explains:

Of course the path we followed was absurd by our government standards and the standards of the news media in the United States. But our actions were not governed by our standards alone; in this instance, as in many others, sovereign nations elsewhere were attempting to conduct their affairs according to their own best interests. When we are involved with those nations, we cannot always have our way.*

Such niceties have not prevented our unilateral action in many other instances, and certainly for much less reason.

In use, "security" is frequently as elastic as it is arbitrary. As noted in chapter One, the Resor and Starbird memoranda were, in effect, "classified" but quickly "declassified" and released in full when the Army's plans for promoting the Sentinel System got into the newspapers. In those same memoranda, purposeful declassification of hitherto secret missiles and missile test facilities was made a part of the promotion program. How frequently, one wonders, does the military take the wraps from other classified material to make its propaganda points?

The word "propaganda" is fitting. Stemming from the title *Congregatio de propaganda fide* (Congregation, or College, for the Propagation of the Faith)—an organization set up in 1623 to train Roman Catholic missionaries—

* New York: Harper & Row, Publishers, 1970, p. 49.

the word through usage over the years has taken on the meaning set forth in *Webster's New International Dictionary* (Second Edition): "Now, often, secret or clandestine dissemination of ideas, information, gossip, or the like, for the purpose of helping, or injuring, a person, an institution, a cause, etc."

As we have seen, there certainly was secrecy involved in the Army's ABM promotion scheme and plans for "clandestine dissemination of . . . information" as well. The ABM example does not stand alone; in many other of its activities the Department of Defense uses the technique of propaganda to sell its point of view to America.

In November 1969, Vice President Spiro T. Agnew in his speech castigating television commentators gave us his view of a "small group of men" who help shape public opinion by deciding what "40 to 50 million Americans will learn of the day's events in the nation and in the world." There is another group of people much larger than that attacked by the Vice President—numbering approximately 2,800—working to shape public opinion.* This group is even less known to the public since its members are never seen or heard directly. It is made up of government employees and military men on active duty whose job is selling the public on the Department of Defense, the individual military services, and their appropriations.

This vast apparatus has grown quietly since World War II, obediently serving the aims of successive Administra-

* In the report submitted to the Senate Appropriations Committee, the Department of Defense raised the number of people to 4,430 apparently anticipating the very large reduction that Congress would approve. It also shows the type of flexibility that exists within the enormous defense budget that permits "miscalculations" of this magnitude.

tions and its own ends at the same time. Apparently its activities do not disturb the Vice President, whose quest for objectivity is directed at Administration critics rather than supporters.

The growth of the apparatus has not been without problems. In early 1949, when the new Department of Defense was still going through the tortuous process of trying to bring the vying armed services under centralized control, Secretary James V. Forrestal abolished the services' separate information offices and ordered that each assign twenty-five officers to carry out information functions in the offices of the Department of Defense. Forrestal's effort failed, for interservice rivalry continued even under centralized control. In the latter days of the Truman Administration, Secretary of the Air Force Thomas K. Finletter, chafing under congressional criticism of his department's public relations activities, abolished the Air Force's Public Information Office, keeping only fifteen officers in headquarters to carry out its functions. According to John Hohenberg, a longtime observer of press and government relationships, Finletter's action had little effect.

"The whole operation went underground," Hohenberg wrote, "with PIO's popping up in strange guises—even as a chaplain in one instance."*

From 1951 to 1959, the Congress in its annual appropriations for the military limited the amount that could be spent on public relations to $2,755,000. According to Hohenberg, the services complied with the spending limit:

* *The News Media: A Journalist Looks at His Profession* (New York: Holt, Rinehart, and Winston, 1968), p. 116.

. . . by specifying that only particular duties could be classified as public relations. They even made out weekly slips giving the total number of hours spent in the "public relations" function—sometimes none at all, sometimes 30 to 45 minutes out of an entire week. It was not considered "public relations" to "answer queries from the public," i.e. respond to a newspaper inquiry, or to draft statements, write speeches, or do so many of the things that are a normal part of a public relations man's duty.*

The congressional restriction on spending was removed in 1959. The exact reasons for the removal probably are to be found somewhere in the voluminous proceedings of the appriations subcommittees involved, but basically they concerned the difficulty of verifying and auditing the fragmented reports of military PR spending. At any rate, in the years between 1959 and 1969, with restraint removed, admitted public relations spending by the military soared to $27,953,000.** This is the total arrived at from figures supplied to me by the Department of Defense and the three services, a fund of the taxpayers' money that compares favorably to advertising budgets of large corporations.

I believe that these figures supplied to me are, to put it mildly, conservative, for they represent less than $10,000 per person employed in the public affairs apparatus. They also do not include the cost of the use of military aircraft, aircraft carriers, and other naval vessels used for junkets by "civic leaders" and other VIP's. They do not include

---

* *Ibid.*, p. 312.

** This figure was raised to $44,062,000 in the report submitted to the Senate Appropriations Committee by the Department of Defense. Again, this and other "miscalculations" mentioned in this book illustrate the leeway existent in the defense budget that can be corrected in anticipation of reductions that Congress might approve.

materials used for troop information programs that find their way into public use. They obviously do not include the overhead costs of the military installations and facilities that are used in the public relations effort.

The military public relations campaign is directed at all of the American people ("targets," they are called in the manuals, a nice military word adopted by Madison Avenue and readopted by military PR people in its new sense). The audience ranges from school children and teachers to ranchers and farmers, from union leaders to defense contractors, from Boy Scouts to American Legionnaires. The principal target of the military PR men, however, is the media. Although Vice President Agnew may decry the influence of the Washington–New York "communications establishment," American public opinion is more largely influenced by local newspapers, radio and television stations. There are more than 1,700 daily newspapers (plus thousands of weeklies), more than 7,200 radio stations, and more than 650 television stations.

These outlets, hungry for material, are supplied by the military with press releases, pictures, tapes, and films produced by the Department of Defense's world-wide publicity apparatus. Each of the services maintains "home town news centers" from which flow stories, taped interviews, film clips, pictures of individual servicemen. The broader aspects of military activities are as thoroughly covered. From Washington and field offices in major cities flow thousands of press releases, augmented by additional thousands from individual commands, posts, and bases.

Radio stations receive military-produced tapes ranging from a report on professional sports to dance music by an

28

Air Force band. Television stations with air time to fill can borrow films from the military, ranging in content from an Army view of "progress" in South Korea to a Navy version of what to do about LSD. The military even produces its own films exclusively for commercial television that favorably treat the "Vietnamization" of the war in Southeast Asia.

Very few Americans, I am convinced, have much cognizance of the extent of the military sell or its effects on their lives through the molding of their opinions, the opinions (and votes on appropriations) of their representatives in the Congress, and the opinions of their presumed ombudsmen in the American press. Even those few who have given serious thought to this matter have had available to them only sparse information about the military information apparatus.

To my knowledge, although this mind-shaping machine has now and then come under attack when its activities were so glaring and obvious that they could not be hidden, and although scholars in the communications field have written learnedly about it, no one has attempted to describe for the general public its parts and standard operating procedures.

3 | The Pentagon

SOME OF US IN THE SENATE who at one time or another have questioned aspects of military activity or spending have often been amazed at the rapidity with which the Pentagon can respond to get out its side of the story. And those of us sensitive to the feelings of our constituents are frequently surprised at the widespread and sometimes adverse response from home that is quickly generated by something we have said that is critical of some weapons system or Pentagon policy.

Until not too long ago I was satisfied to chalk up these happenings to the promotional activities of the public relations men of defense-oriented corporations, to veterans groups, and to what I thought was a relative handful of Pentagon press men. I know now how wrong I was.

When Congress passed the National Security Act in 1947, it voted to end the rampant rivalry among the military services and to require each to subordinate its parochial interests to those of the military establishment as a whole. But here we are twenty-three years later with the Army, Navy, and Air Force each spending millions of tax dollars annually on persuasion of the public that its particular brand of weaponry is the best. Competition for the public's affections—and their representatives' votes in Congress—rivals the hucksterism of detergent manufacturers. This is hardly the conduct the public deserves from organizations that, taken together, consume almost half of all federal revenue.

Besides the millions spent by the separate services on publicity, other millions are spent by the office of the Secretary of Defense itself in its role as coordinator of military information and as a purveyor, too. The department's public relations apparatus consists of 200 military persons and civilians who cost the taxpayers $3,431,000* in salaries last year, plus $266,000 in ancillary expenses. What the total expenditure would be if operating expenses, overhead, and other costs absorbed by other accounts within the multibillion-dollar defense budget were included can only be surmised.

These 200** people operate under the Assistant Secretary of Defense for Public Affairs, a post currently held by Daniel Z. Henkin. He is responsible under Department of Defense Directive 5122.5 of July 5, 1969, for running "an integrated DoD [Department of Defense] public affairs program which will: (1) Provide the American people with *maximum* information about the Department of Defense

---

* Later reduced in the report to the Senate Appropriations Committee to a total of $3,403,000.

** Later raised in the report to the Senate Appropriations Committee to 218.

consistent with national security. (2) *Initiate and support* activities contributing toward good relations between the Department of Defense and all segments of the public at home and abroad." [Italics mine.]

There is little doubt that the Department of Defense and the separate services are hard at work providing positive information to the American public and initiating and supporting activities to build up good public relations, but these efforts, in my view, are more designed to persuade the American people that the military is "good for you" than genuinely to inform.

The Office of the Assistant Secretary for Public Affairs is the basic source of news about the military establishment. This office performs a proper and necessary activity, but its total operations range far beyond press releases and press conferences. In scope they range from:

1. Five television news crews in Southeast Asia covering "feature aspects" of the Vietnam war for distribution to commercial television stations in the United States;*

2. to a speakers bureau that provided 492 high-ranking military officers and civilian officials to organizations throughout the country in Fiscal Year 1969;

3. to a Magazine and Book Branch that acts as a literary agent, seeking out commercial markets for material written by members of the armed services;

4. to an Organizations Division that maintains liaison with 500 defense-oriented private groups, including veterans organizations, and mails material to 287 of them on a regular basis;

5. to a Projects Division that schedules everything

* Discussed in chapter 7.

from parachute jumpers and aerobatic teams to marching bands and color guards for fairs, celebrations, and other public events.

One Pentagon service intrigued me. Its Audio-Visual News Branch produces something called "Spotmaster," described as similar to Dial-the-Weather, that provides the latest Defense Department news releases in audio form to anyone in Washington dialing OXford 5-6201.

Until last year, the Defense Department had another project worth pondering. Although the Department of State is supposedly responsible for cultural exchanges, Defense with State, the United States Information Agency, and the White House, sponsored tours of this country by foreign journalists. Between 1966 and 1969, about 200 of them were brought here from Europe, Africa, South and East Asia, and the Pacific. Tranportation within the United States was by military aircraft, and a large proportion of the stops made were at military installations.

The Defense Department has extraordinary resources that permit it to transport American as well as foreign visitors about the country—as in the Army's "Operation Understanding." By going into the community, picking local leaders, flying them to military facilities, and briefing them on chosen, specific subjects, it is able to propagandize and influence attitudes toward these activities.

Each service has its own civilian tour program, but the most prestigious is the Joint Civilian Orientation Conference—an eight-day tour for seventy civilians run by the Office of the Secretary of Defense. These tours have been going on since the early 1950s, and until 1968 were made in chartered passenger aircraft from commercial airlines. (The cost of the 1967 charter was $19,157.) Now military aircraft are used and the cost information is no longer available.

According to the Defense Department, a "conference" accomplishes these objectives: "It opens the Department of Defense to public inspection; it responds to the desire of key Americans to maintain an interest in and an understanding of their federal government; it gives members of the Armed Forces and private citizens an opportunity to know and understand each other better; it offers a means for an exchange of ideas; and it helps explain the disposition of the Defense dollar."

"Defense dollars"—or better, "taxpayers' dollars"—are lavished on these trips with the expensive might of the military machine put on full-dress display for the civilian visitors. (A good percentage of the visitors come from defense industries and no doubt assist in influencing the views of their fellow participants.) Tour itineraries vary from year to year; a representative one might include a briefing at the Pentagon; a flight to Strategic Air Command headquarters in Nebraska, with a demonstration of air-refueling of a B-52 en route; a stop at the underground headquarters of the North American Air Defense Command in Colorado; a stop at Cape Kennedy to see NASA's facilities, but also to see Air Force activity there; a firepower demonstration by artillery and aircraft at Fort Bragg, North Carolina, plus a visit to the Special Forces ("Green Berets") Training Center; a Marine Corps assault landing from the sea on the North Carolina beaches; a tour of Navy facilities at Norfolk, Virginia, before a helicopter flight to an aircraft

35

carrier in the Atlantic; demonstrations of carrier operations, bombing, and anti-submarine warfare; and finally another Pentagon briefing, this one by the Secretary or Under Secretary of Defense and the Joint Chiefs of Staff.

A participant in one of the tours, a man who describes himself as "somewhat hawkish," said he returned home with mixed feelings about what he had seen and about the VIP treatment he had received.

"The trip was truly impressive," he said, "and it was very informative. I learned a lot, and I think the rest of my group would say the same. But what it all must have cost bothers me. Generals and admirals and officers of all ranks dropped whatever they were doing to accommodate us. We not only had briefings everywhere, but we also had a chance to talk to the top people singly or in groups, and, of course, we were very well entertained.

"The demonstrations we saw throughout were thrilling —I suppose chilling is a better word. At Fort Bragg it was one of an infantry battalion in the attack, supported by artillery and aircraft. First the planes came in shooting their rockets, dropping bombs, and then napalm making great billowing bursts of flame. Artillery pounded the area, and the infantrymen then fired mortars and machine guns before moving up against the 'enemy.' We watched all this from about three-quarters of a mile away, sitting in bleachers on a hill, under a canvas canopy with soft drinks and toilets available. That night the commanding general had a cocktail party for us with the top brass, and then a sitdown dinner with a damned good wine served with it.

"The Bragg demonstration obviously had been scheduled,

for there were a number of foreign military attachés there and what I would guess were student officers from somewhere. But several of the other demonstrations—the one the Navy put on at sea I think, in particular—were staged for our benefit. I just wonder if impressing 70 supposedly important people was worth the time and money expended."

The civilian guests themselves have to spend comparatively little. Although the Defense Department's official description of the "conference" says that "participants pay all of their own expenses, including food, lodging, and entertainment," as most of the overnight stops are made at military installations where military rates are charged for food and room, the total bill is small. The participant quoted above said he spent $138 of his own money. He lives in Washington so he had no transportation costs as did those participants who lived in other parts of the country.

After the tours are over, the participants are encouraged to join an organization of "alumni" called the Defense Orientation Conference Association. The association, which has been in existence since 1952 and has 850 members, maintains a Washington office, keeps the members informed of things military, and gathers them together annually in Washington for a meeting and a formal dinner-dance. Attendance is reported to be good.

The Defense Department does not restrict its attempts to influence public opinion to taking people from their home towns and showing them what is being done with the "Defense dollar" at military installations. It vigorously carries its propaganda programs into local communities as well. These programs can take many forms, as we have already seen and as will be seen in later pages, but there is one program that I would like to touch on here—the military's essays into "education."

In 1961, my attention was called to an extensive program of "alerts," "seminars," "freedom forums," "strategy for survival conferences," and other meetings with resounding titles being held throughout the country to alert the public to the menace of the cold war. They seemed to have stemmed from a National Security Council directive of 1958 that called on the military to play a role in arousing the public to its danger. Unfortunately, the programs put military officers on the same platforms with exponents of the radical right and in appearance, at least, the meetings were assisted and supported by the Pentagon. Reserve officers attending the sessions, for example, were given retirement credit for the time spent listening to the speeches and discussions. In addition, the basic approach of the seminars was developed by anticommunist speakers in cooperation with the National War College, the most prestigious of the services' "post-graduate" institutions.

Among the objectives of one such program, a "Fourth Dimensional Warfare Seminar" in Pittsburgh, Pennsylvania, on April 15, 1961, were:

"To provide guidance to military reservists and to selected civic and business leaders regarding the deceptive Communist subversive efforts being directed toward the United States . . . To reveal areas of Communist influence upon American youth through infiltration into the theater, motion picture, television, and other entertainment media."

This program was sponsored by the Greater Pittsburgh Chamber of Commerce "in cooperation with various military organizations in the Pittsburgh area." Two generals and their staffs were thanked for "assistance and support" in the seminar brochure.

After examining a report of the Pittsburgh seminar and of ten others around the country, including two in my state of Arkansas, I was prompted to send a memorandum to the then Secretary of Defense, Robert S. McNamara. In this memorandum I said:

"Fundamentally, it is believed that the American people have little, if any, need to be alerted to the menace of the cold war. Rather, the need is for understanding of the true nature of that menace and the direction of the public's present and foreseeable awareness of the fact of the menace toward support of the President's own total program for survival in a nuclear age. There are no reasons to believe that military personnel generally can contribute to this need beyond their specific technical competence to explain their own role. On the contrary, there are many reasons and some evidence for believing that an effort by the military, beyond this limitation, involves considerable danger."

I recommended to Secretary McNamara that the cold war activities of the military be examined by the Executive branch, and that controls be instituted as necessary. The reaction of many to my memorandum was that I was trying to "muzzle the military," and for a time this became a subject of controversy.

Although military participation in the "alerts," "seminars," and the rest of the speaking programs espousing the hard anticommunist line subsequently faded away, there remained another military-sponsored "educational" program, similar in organization if not in aim, that is still operating today. This is the National Security Seminar conducted by the Industrial College of the Armed Forces, another of the Pentagon's "post-graduate" schools.

The Statement of Mission of the Industrial College of the Armed Forces reads:

"To conduct courses of study in the economic and industrial aspects of national security and in the management of resources under all conditions, giving due consideration to the interrelated military, political, and social factors affecting national security, and in the context of national and world affairs, in order to enhance the preparation of selected military officers and key civilian personnel for important staff, command, and policy-making positions in the national and international security structure."

There undoubtedly is a need for an institution such as the industrial college to train military officers and upper level Foreign Service officers of the Department of State and the United States Information Agency in the complexities of the jobs they have to do. But there seems to me to be no earthly reason why the industrial college should also extend its educative process to the general public, which, in effect, is what it does with the National Security Seminar.

Since 1948, the industrial college has sent teams of military officers around the country to run two-week programs based on the material used to train students in the regular course at Fort McNair in Washington, D.C. Ostensibly, the courses are for reserve officers of the military services, who get credit for retirement by attending, but the larger number of participants are drawn from the general public, and the sponsors in almost all cases in recent years have been local Chambers of Commerce. The promotion sheet distributed to arouse interest in the seminars says they "bring to a community an educational program with no counterpart in government, industry, business, or the field of education. It is designed to inform, to enhance understanding, and to encourage participation by the individual in community, state, and national affairs."

The seminars are heavily larded with discussions of foreign affairs covering such topics as Africa, South Asia, Comparative Political Systems, Geopolitics, International Economics, Communist China, and World Agriculture. The contents of those of the lectures that I have reviewed present a simplistic, often outdated, and factually incorrect view of complex world problems. The poor quality of the lectures alone is sufficient justification for abolishing the program. But the real issue is of far more fundamental importance. It is not a proper function of the Department of Defense to educate civilians on foreign policy issues or to teach them to be better citizens, even if the material presented is completely objective, which is frequently not the case.

An Anchorage, Alaska, man who attended one of the seminars wrote to me objecting to the approach taken by the speakers.

"Charges," he wrote, "were made at every opportunity against most liberal activities on university campuses and at one point condemnations were made of what were referred to as 'skeptical congressional powers.' Outbursts of applause followed charged comments about social disruption and personal testimonials were made by the civilians on the floor of the auditorium after the speakers had effectively silenced a man asking about disarmament. At several points what could be called nothing else but 'scare tactics' were

41

used to intimate that long lead [preparation] time considerations necessitated immediately the increase of our nuclear arsenal and strategic bomber squadrons. The C-5-A cost overruns were pooh-poohed as 'just one of those things'. . . . The seminar did suggest one important thing to me. The greatest threat to American national security is the American Military Establishment and the no-holds-barred type of logic it uses to justify its zillion dollar existence."

Since 1948, teams from the Industrial College of the Armed Forces have conducted National Security Seminars in more than 170 cities—from El Paso, Texas, to Duluth, Minnesota, and from Portland, Maine, to San Francisco, California—before audiences totaling more than 180,000 persons. The operators of the seminars try to make them self-germinating. In the 617-page course outline the participants receive, a message from the director of the Seminar School asks participants to "communicate with your friends and associates in future seminar cities and encourage their attendance." The director's message also says, "Contact your local Chamber of Commerce or other potential local sponsor and suggest that the Seminar be invited to your community; a letter to the Commandant of the College will suffice to indicate a community's interest."

Those who have attended the seminars are asked to form "alumni groups to continue the association and informal study of current affairs begun at the Seminar."

"Many individuals," the message goes on to say, "have developed their own presentations and carried the word to service clubs and other organizations. Others have voiced their opinion on matters of special concern in 'letters to the editor.' Parents have discussed Seminar topics with their children and thus bridged part of the gap between generations."*

All of the seminar lectures are put on tape and can be borrowed for sixty days; if permanent taped copies are desired, the participants can send tapes to the Industrial College of the Armed Forces and the desired speeches will be recorded on them—two speeches on each 1,200-foot tape. In addition, the college offers free to the participants a correspondence course, "National Security Management," described as "a graduate-level course providing an appreciation of the interrelated military, logistical, administrative, scientific, technological, political, and social factors as they affect national security."

According to the Defense Department, the seminars program costs only about $35,000 a year, besides the pay and allowances of the military officers participating; Chambers of Commerce, for the most part, foot the bill, and civilian participants pay to attend the sessions. Within the enormous outlays for defense, the cost is of little consequence, but the presumptuousness of the military to assume the role of educators of people in Yakima, Washington, Provo, Utah, Columbia, South Carolina, and Gainesville, Florida, about "Communist China and U.S. Security" or "United States in World Affairs" or "Comparative Political Systems" is of grave consequence and should be stopped.

The military's "education" activities are but a small part of the total effort the Department of Defense expends on the citizenry. Like any organization of high visibility, it has

---

* My Alaskan correspondent said that high school students invited to one of the seminar sessions in Anchorage "snickered" at the military speakers' explanation of our role in Vietnam.

to worry about "community relations." The presence of large military installations and large numbers of military personnel in populated localities naturally cause day-to-day problems with local governments and local residents for, whatever economic advantage may accrue due to the presence of the military near a community, the demands put upon them are burdensome. Community relations programs obviously are necessary. But, as with so many of its activities, the Defense Department carries "community relations" far beyond what would seem to be necessary. Possibly it does so because of the normal panache of the military, but the more likely reason is the enormous resources at its disposal.

The Pentagon can pick up a town's leading citizens and fly them to Florida or California. It can provide generals and admirals whose names make the headlines as speakers for the local Kiwanis Club or Chamber of Commerce. Military units and bands and color guards are available for celebrations. Skydiving paratroopers can enliven the county fair. Towns with deep water harbors can be visited by impressive Navy ships, open to public visiting. Local high schools can have ROTC units equipped and supported. And all at no expense to the local citizen—except in his tax bill.

Department of Defense Directive 5410.18 of February 9, 1968, defines a "Community Relations Program" as "that command function which evaluates public attitudes, identifies the mission of a military organization with the public interest, and executes a program of action to earn public understanding and acceptance." The activities to be carried on are listed in interesting order: "liaison and cooperation

44

with industry, with industrial, technical and trade associations, with labor" lead all the rest. (Until a year or so ago, the Office of the Assistant Secretary of Defense for Public Affairs each month published a magazine titled *Defense Industry Bulletin,* described in the Community Relations Directive "as a means of direct communication with the industrial community." It has been taken over by the Defense Supply Agency, a more appropriate organization— if it is appropriate to have such a close military-industrial connection.)

The expressed purposes of military community relations programs stretch beyond what would seem to be their normal purview. Besides "developing public understanding of and cooperation with the DoD in its community relations program" and "assisting recruiting," the purposes include "informing the public on the state of preparedness of the DoD" and "promoting national security and stimulating patriotic spirit." The multi-million-dollar public relations programs conducted by the Pentagon and the services apparently are not enough to keep people informed. As for "stimulating patriotic spirit," in our present-day society where patriotism seems to be equated with approval of billions for defense and where superpatriotism is burgeoning, it seems to me that the military is reaching too far.

Of considerable importance to the Defense Department in selling the military point of view is the stream of American citizens who pass through terms of military service. We have become a nation of veterans—now more than 28 million. This means that more than one-fifth of our adult population has been subjected to some degree of indoctrination in military values and attitudes. And all have

45

been, whether they liked it or not, that dream of the public relations man—a captive audience.

The Pentagon today has a captive audience numbering more than 3 million Americans in uniform, and a very large part of Defense Department information activity is directed at them, although not charged to general public relations activities. The responsibility of reaching this audience, in large part, rests with the Office of Information for the Armed Forces, a part of the Office of the Assistant Secretary of Defense (Manpower and Reserve Affairs). The purposes of this office, according to the Defense Department, are "to help the commander insure that the military men and women are fully informed in order that they may (1) comprehend the values of our Government and our American Heritage; (2) be fully aware of the threat to free nations; (3) understand ideologies inimical to the free institutions upon which the United States is founded; and (4) realize the responsibilities and objectives of the individual military citizen."

All of the members of the armed forces are exposed to programs furthering these ends throughout their periods of service, and the 1.5 million stationed overseas beyond the normal sources of information available at home are a truly captive audience.

For soldiers, sailors, and airmen abroad the news from home—and the news of what is happening in the world—comes from the Office of Information for the Armed Forces. Last year it sent to military units 8.5 million copies of 70 publications, 104,000 clip sheets for service newspapers, and 1.5 million posters, but its largest effort was put into the Armed Forces Radio and Television Service. AFRTS, as it is known, is the world's largest television and radio network under single control. Its land-based facilities consist of 204 radio stations and 80 television stations, extending from Thailand eastward around the world to Iran, and it has 56 radio stations and 11 television stations on Navy ships at sea. Troops in Vietnam are served by 6 AM and 5 FM radio stations and 6 television stations. There are 68 radio stations in Europe and 10 television stations, some in both categories of such high power that they blanket their areas. One television station in Iran serves fewer than 800 servicemen, but many Iranians, it is reported, have adapters on their TV sets so that they can watch the latest fare from the American television networks. The cost of operating this network, without including associated military salaries, runs into the tens of millions of dollars annually.

Programming costs, however, are relatively small, since ABC, CBS, and NBC provide videotapes of their entertainment programs free to AFRTS's Los Angeles office for distribution world-wide. For its radio programming, both news and entertainment, AFRTS draws on the three major networks, the Mutual Broadcasting System, Metromedia, and the Sports Network, and for news has the network output plus that of the Associated Press and United Press International.

With this enormous amount of programming available—450,000 radio program transcriptions and 60 million feet of TV film annually—it would seem that the serviceman abroad would be very well served and very well informed. He is well served—by entertainment, for entertainment makes up the bulk of the broadcasts. But the news he gets first has to go through several military sieves before it

47

reaches the uniformed listener or viewer overseas, and the sievers are people conditioned by the purposes of the Office of Information for the Armed Forces described above.

Early this year an Army enlisted man who broadcast news in Vietnam charged that he had been "censored." Representative John E. Moss, who heads the House Subcommittee on Government Information, investigated the matter and decided that there had been no censorship, but that more precise guidelines should be laid down for military broadcasters. Writing about the incident this past spring, a former Army newsman agreed that there was no censorship on the Armed Forces Vietnam Network, but "the news comes out just sounding censored." AFRTS possibly cannot be accused even of this venial sin, but it still controls the flow of information to a large number of Americans who depend on it to form their opinions and to know what is really going on. And AFRTS is 100 percent military. The potential danger of its misuse is more than a little disturbing.

4 | The Navy: From Mahan to Moorer

THE UNITED STATES NAVY has a well-filled pantheon of heroes, ranging from John Paul Jones to "Bull" Halsey, on whose fame and exploits the traditions of the service have been built. However, today's globe-ranging fleet and current Navy policy probably depend as much on a well-known Navy historian as on any of its heroes.

This historian was Rear Admiral Alfred Thayer Mahan, whose writings provided Theodore Roosevelt, the elder Henry Cabot Lodge, and others at the turn of the century with the rationale that involved the United States in the far reaches of the western Pacific and committed the country to a "big navy" policy.

In 1890, Mahan published a book titled *Influence of Sea Power on History, 1660–1783* based on lectures he had made at the Naval War College in Newport, Rhode Island. In this work, and in subsequent writings, Mahan argued that seapower controlled the destiny of nations and brought national power and prosperity by making possible expanded foreign commerce. His writings, in large measure, created a demand for a larger Navy, brought about a change in Navy strategic principles, and profoundly affected naval thinking around the world. But the influence of Mahan was felt in more than seapower and naval construction; the ideas he expressed gave the self-righteous mercantile imperialists of the period moral justification for their actions.

More than a quarter of a century ago, Merle Curti in his book *The Growth of American Thought* analyzed Mahan's influence on these people with observations that could be applied to American policy of the past twenty years.

Evil being inherent in the world [Curti wrote], the righteous nations, which could never submit questions of national honor and interest to arbitration, must use force to curb evil and to promote well-being in the commonwealth of the world. The moral nation, the powerful nation, must, in short, be responsible for the triumph of morality on earth . . . Mahan, whose faith in God and His righteousness was deep, believed that if adequate preparations had been made by the nation espousing good, if sufficient sacrifices were undergone, if inner discipline and morals were what they should be, God would never permit a just cause to go down in defeat.*

Shortly before the Spanish-American War began, Mahan wrote, "Whether they will or no, Americans must now begin to look outward." Unlike many philosophers, he lived to see his words become action. We arrogated to ourselves the problems in the Philippines; we occupied Cuba; we added Hawaii, Guam, Wake, American Samoa, Puerto Rico, and

* New York: Harper & Brothers, Publishers, 1943, p. 672.

the Isthmus of Panama to our territory within the course of a few years. Mahan's "big navy" policy had to be followed to protect these far-flung possessions, and we started on our way to becoming a great naval power. Today, of course, we have the greatest fleet of warships, but Navy men, still influenced by Mahan, want us to become greater. To attain this end, the one Navy writer of 1890 has become thousands.

Each year the Secretary of the Navy sets forth the public relations objectives to be sought by his department. In 1969 the Secretary's goals included "gaining the understanding and support of American citizens" for "the need for modern ships, aircraft, and equipment throughout the Naval Service." To justify the billions required for these "ships, aircraft, and equipment," the public was to be duly warned of "the challenge of the continued growth of Soviet seapower and its expanding worldwide operations."

In order to gain "the understanding and support" of Americans, the Navy in Fiscal Year 1969 maintained a public relations apparatus consisting of a full-time staff of 1,086* plus 1,600 to 1,800 working at the activity part-time on ships and shore installations. Identifiable costs supplied to me by the Navy for that year were $9,901,000.** Both the expenditures and the number of personnel involved are the largest reported by the three armed services. In Washington alone, the Navy's Office of Information employs 147 people with a budget of $1,745,000. Parkinson's Law seems to

---

* Later raised to 1,800 in the report to the Senate Appropriations Committee.

** Later raised to $14,340,000 (Marine Corps included).

51

work in the Navy; the overall budget has gone up 25 percent in the past three years and the Washington operation is up 57 percent in staff and 65 percent in costs for the same period.

In addition to the public relations efforts of uniformed men on active duty and civilian employees, the Navy message is spread throughout the country by thirty-one very active Naval Reserve Public Affairs Companies, consisting of 409 officers and six enlisted men—some of the companies based in such unlikely "Navy towns" as Sioux City, Iowa, and Topeka, Kansas.

To direct the promotional activities of all of these people, the Navy with typical thoroughness promulgates minutely detailed plans for each of its commands and bureaus. The plans for 1968, which I placed in the *Congressional Record,* filled nearly nineteen columns in tiny agate type. The Navy's Bureau of Medicine and Surgery's PR plan, which includes more than eighty projects, runs from publicizing medical support of the forces in Vietnam to promoting the medical aspects of "Operation Deep Freeze" in Antarctica. The Bureau of Personnel intended to mark the first anniversary of the appointment of the Master Chief Petty Officer of the Navy and the commissioning of the Naval Training Station at Orlando, Florida. Under "Worldwide Naval Operations and Versatility" was listed the item "Growth and Expanding Operations of the Soviet Navy," with the statement, "Events indicate the Soviet Navy, increasing in number and quality of ships, plans to deploy more fleet units beyond its coastal areas. It is necessary to develop public understanding of the nature of this change in its sea-power from a largely continental one, with naval operations in coastal waters, to one not limited to the Eurasian continents. Its activities now include more widespread operations, including operations adjacent to the territorial waters of the United States." A long section—forty-two projects in all—is devoted to a suggested list of activities which the Naval Reserve Public Affairs Companies were encouraged to undertake. Among the proposals from Navy Washington headquarters were the following:

If local radio, TV, and newspapers are favorable to Navy news call them up from time to time and tell them how much people like getting the Navy news.

If the news is devoid of Navy activity, call the media and ask the simple question, "Where is the Navy news today?"*

It could be that the Navy feels such importuning is necessary in its competition with the Army and the Air Force for public attention and public funds. Excepting the Marine Corps—and few civilians connect the Marines with the Navy Department—the Navy has had a relatively less conspicuous role in the Vietnam fighting. Activities of carrier aircraft, Seabee construction battalions, and "riverine forces" rarely get publicity, for the war is dominated by the other services. (This, however, relieves the Navy from heavy casualties and keeps it from being involved in atrocity stories.) As a consequence, in defense public relations efforts, the Navy's global reach and the asserted threat of

* The Army takes an entirely different tack in the handling of editors. Its "Army Information Officers' Guide" lists among "don'ts": "Don't thank the editor, publisher, program director, and bureau chief for using your releases. If the story is news, they are glad to get it."

Soviet seapower are subordinated to the realities of Southeast Asia.

Public attention to the Navy's world-wide role is needed, for maintaining the enormous fleet its proponents want is very expensive and must have justification. As an example, by the time the nuclear-powered carrier *CVAN 69* is completed, its cost may be as much as $700 million because of "overruns." The newest non-nuclear carrier with the fleet, the U.S.S. *John F. Kennedy,* cost $277 million; and converting the U.S.S. *Midway* for modern operations cost $202 million, more than twice what was spent on its construction twenty-five years ago. In addition, the costs of operating carriers and of providing the other ships needed to support and protect them are incredibly high.

Six years ago, before the "blips" appeared on the radar screens of the destroyers *Maddox* and *Turner Joy* in the Tonkin Gulf, the Navy was spending several billions of dollars more each year than was the Army, a service with twice as many men. Even with the astronomical costs of the kind of land warfare we are waging in Vietnam, the Navy's expenditures in Fiscal Year 1969 were $22,507,495,249, only about $2 billion less than the Army's for the same year.

To keep alive support for such an enormous expenditure, a large promotional effort is required. Among some of the 1969 facets of that effort reported to me by Navy officials were:

1. One thousand one hundred thirty-six news releases prepared by the Navy's Office of Information's News Branch in Washington;

2. Thirty-nine thousand photos distributed to news media;

3. Forty-nine news films prepared for TV use on subjects ranging from Russian trawlers off Virginia to the retirement of a Navy seaplane;

4. Fifty-five one-minute TV "news featurettes" on subjects such as civic action in Vietnam and Navy operations off Latin America;

5. Navy assistance in production of about twelve commercial films;

6. Assistance in producing some 100 non-commercial films, primarily for Navy contractors;

7. Operation of a speakers bureau in Washington of top civilian and uniformed personnel which filled 251 speaking engagements across the country.

These examples are only representative and largely concern Washington efforts. *Direction* is a monthly Navy magazine that goes to all public relations personnel and commanding officers. In its November 1968 issue, *Direction* included an article summarizing the Navy's publicity activities in Fiscal Year 1968. (No similar summary was published for FY 69.)

One constant problem in public affairs is measuring results. Finding a "ruler" to measure results of efforts expended is not an easy or exact business. However, there are certain Fiscal Year 1968 public affairs accomplishments that have been logged by CHINFO (Office of the Chief of Information). The following summary of some of the major CHINFO-monitored or sponsored programs gives all hands a better idea of what has been done at home to gain more recognition for the outstanding job being done in the Fleet.

NAVY PUBLIC AFFAIRS FY 68

Event	Audiences Reached
Armed Forces Day Open Houses	770,000
SecNav Guest Cruise Program	560
Boy Scout Cruises	2,500
President's Youth Opportunity Program	51,326
Blue Angels*	6,415,189
Navy/USMC Speakers (145 events)	370,000
Other Community Relations Events	2,650,000
(316 programs)	
Total Audience Reached	10,259,575

Navy public affairs activities have not diminished since Fiscal Year 1968, so it can be assumed—from more recent articles in *Direction* and other information supplied by the Navy—that audiences today are as large if not larger than they were in 1968.

The program of one of the Navy reserve public affairs companies gives an idea of these activities by just a part-time organization. The company, NRPAC 9-2, is in Chicago and describes itself as "uniquely suited through size, geographic location, and membership background to carry out Navy-oriented public affairs activities in the fertile and important midwest area." Its 1969 plan called for "the use of every available communications medium to bring the story of the Navy and Navy reserve to targeted audiences. This includes: print media, newspapers, trade magazines, Sunday supplements; direct mail; personal contact; broadcast, TV and radio; advertising, brochures, outdoor billboards, and electronic devices; and others."

* Naval aerobatics team; the Air Force has a similar demonstration group.

To make use of all of these public relations tools, the company listed more than 40 projects in its plan. They ranged from publicizing "Navy Sabbath" and arranging that the "Navy Hymn" be sung in 4,000-odd Chicago area churches to producing a 13-week radio show for use on Station WGN; from working in conjunction with the *Chicago Tribune* on a special awards program for persons and organizations displaying the American flag* to arranging cruises for members of the Chicago Press Club aboard Navy ships stationed in the Great Lakes.

One of the Chicago company's activities had the attributes of old-fashioned press agentry: "Set up a project to aid 'Hands Across the Sea' program by providing six tons of chewing gum from the Wrigley Company for the Navy to distribute in Spanish-speaking countries. Publicize movement and distribution of gum."

The Navy generally is more subtle in its approach to public relations than the Chicago reservists' attempt at Wrigleyization of Latin America. Impressive cruises on aircraft carriers and other large naval vessels is more in its line. The public relations reserve companies are asked to nominate the participants in these cruises—nominees being defined as "top media executives for yearly trips to Hawaii (fifteen per trip) on an aircraft carrier and return via Navy air to West Coast" and "outstanding leaders of the area for Global Strategy Discussions at the Naval War College, VIP cruises, and other special orientation cruises."

* Promotion of the display of the National Flag is one of the Navy's service-wide public affairs projects. It is laudable enough *if* it remains unconnected with the current campaign of superpatriots that equates the display of flag decals on automobile windows with love of country and unlimited support for the war in Vietnam.

57

The junkets at sea apparently at times are used to pay off "top media executives" if the manner of selection in Sioux City is any indication. A Sioux City Navy reserve company project reads: "Contact with media personnel and selection of those most closely cooperating." Cooperation obviously means beating the Navy's tub. Hundreds of people outside the field of journalism enjoy the hospitality of "the Secretary of the Navy's Guest Cruise Program," usually a four-day trip to Pearl Harbor. There were thirteen such cruises in 1968 and 1969, with participants ranging from sheep rancher to steel magnate to labor leader. During the voyage and the stay in Hawaii, these people, under the most favorable circumstances, get a thorough indoctrination about the Navy's power and the Navy's needs.

The size and majesty of a huge aircraft carrier pushing through the bright blue Pacific can help make believers of almost anyone. The *Washington Monthly* in an article critical of the Navy's carrier mentality earlier this year said, "One of the carrier opponents in the Senate remarked privately to another, 'Don't ever go aboard one of those things and watch air operations at sea—you'll get so charged up, you'll vote for every nuclear carrier they try to slide into the pipeline.' "*

One of the Secretary of the Navy's recent guests on a carrier cruise—a professional man of stature—when asked about his trip was enthusiastic in his admiration of the Navy.

"Civilians are just not aware of the role the Navy is playing and of the might it has under its control," he said.

* John Wicklein, "The Navy Prepares for World War II," *Washington Monthly*, February, 1970, p. 10.

"I know I wasn't until I made this trip. The ability of the Navy to move its ships and planes almost anywhere at the moment they are needed is fantastic."

This guest said that the Navy "had a full agenda for us everywhere." The activities included a reception by Admiral John S. McCain, Jr., commander of all U.S. forces in the Pacific, a submarine trip out of Pearl Harbor, and a demonstration of the Navy's air capability in a flight by jet transport from Hawaii to the West Coast.

"I was impressed," the guest said.

Considerably more sophisticated than the glamor cruises to Hawaii is the annual "Global Strategy Discussion," a cerebral exercise put on at the Naval War College in Newport, Rhode Island, where Mahan held forth in the latter part of the nineteenth century. The guest lists for these "discussions" are possibly even more carefully put together than the Defense Department's "Joint Civilian Orientation Conferences." The participants in 1968 ranged from the board chairman of Woodward and Lothrop, Washington's largest department store, to the president of the Defense Department-financed "think tank," the Hudson Institute. All in all, the flavor of the invitation list was distinctly that of a board meeting of the military-industrial complex. Some of the defense industries represented included Raytheon, Litton, Curtiss-Wright, North American Rockwell, Sikorsky, Lockheed, Bendix, Sperry Rand, General Electric, Aerojet-General, Morrison-Knudson, Martin Marietta, Boeing, and International Business Machines. Undoubtedly the Navy's message on the importance of sea power did not fall on unsympathetic ears.

Even participants who are not of the military-industrial

complex and are even unsympathetic to the military point of view can be impressed by the quality of the Navy's presentation at Newport. One such person, a newspaper publisher, said of the sessions he attended: "You have to give those Navy people credit. They're damned bright. Their presentation was excellent, and their approach to the whole problem of the global strategy the United States should pursue was very persuasive. You have to keep remembering all of the time, as I tried to, that they are trying to sell you a bill of goods—more money, more ships, more things. If you don't remember what's behind their pitch, you're lost."

The careful and intelligent attention paid to the VIP's who take the cruises and attend the discussions is, of course, important for the Navy's image-building efforts, for these people, by and large, are what the public relations man calls "opinion-molders." But the larger part of the service's effort goes into plain old-fashioned public relations, using such gimmicks as stunt-flying aircraft, band concerts, and "soft sell" television advertising.

Direction has articles on the use of aircraft and the "soft sell" on facing pages in its issue of February 1969. The first is primarily concerned with the problems of meeting the requirements of Navy Regulations in setting up a "flyover" by the Blue Angels or other Navy planes. The second article, "Telling the Story—Softly," waxes eloquent about the possibilities of selling the Navy on free television time.

"The camera comes in low and slow," the article begins, "revealing a young girl kicking a small object in the sand. Then she turns and looks out over the ocean. We hear the ocean and the lapping waves and the sound of a lone sea gull. Then the sound effects go under for a low-key narration.

"This is one of a series of the Navy's new soft-sell spots which began in September. . . . By telling its story with TV spots the Navy has taken a page from *Fortune* magazine, which noted that large companies received higher profits when they invested more of their advertising budgets in spot television."

The Navy doesn't have to worry about expenditure, except for the cost of producing the films. Local radio stations use the spots to fill "public service" time on their daily programs. Most of the scripts for the films, *Direction* says, have been written by Albert C. Brook, University of Nebraska journalism professor, who "pioneered successful soft-sell messages like 'Better Things for Better Living—Through Chemistry.' "

"His series of award-winning announcements for Du Pont," the article goes on to say, "overcame public relations problems similar to those facing the Navy—lack of thorough understanding resulting in an outdated image of an extremely large organization."

The Navy's television effort is by no means limited to spot announcements. There is an audio-visual branch in the Navy Office of the Chief of Information that maintains liaison with more than 600 television stations and 5,000 radio stations—and competes with the other armed services, which have similar organizations, for free air time. The Navy's audio-visual office, according to *Direction,* has "placed films on stations in every corner of the country."

The hundreds of films the Navy has for use on television

61

are available for public showing as well. There are at least 240 prints of each of them, and they are available at Navy offices throughout the country. "Experience has shown," the Navy says, "that many of the films in the Naval District libraries are in constant demand by private citizens and organizations."

These films range in subject matter from *Why Vietnam?*, an historically false, blatant piece of propaganda, to two films on the drug problem, *LSD* and *A Trip to No Where*. The latter pair have been recommended for wide public usage by the Department of Justice and are used by the Food and Drug Administration for showing to educators and law enforcement officials. According to the Navy, 510 copies of the *LSD* film are in circulation, and 1,443 of *A Trip to No Where*, and the Navy brags that the films have been seen by more than 75 million persons.

Without doubt there is a serious drug problem in the country and films to combat the evil need to be made, but they should have been made by the Department of Health, Education, and Welfare or the Department of Justice rather than the Navy, whose function has nothing to do with public health, education, or law enforcement.

As for the *Why Vietnam?* film, if the public is to be indoctrinated by its government on controversial foreign policy issues—a highly questionable effort in the first instance —the Department of State would seem to be the agency to do it. But the Navy cannot be singled out among the armed services for carrying its public relations activities far beyond the area of its competence and responsibility. All of the services do the same thing, and do it much too frequently.

In the Navy film catalogue supplied to me is one title

that undoubtedly has since been removed, *The American Dreadnought—U.S.S. New Jersey*. This film depicts the battleship that was brought out of mothballs in 1968 to bombard the Vietnamese coast with its sixteen-inch guns but was put back in mothballs a year later. Refitting and operations cost for that one year of operation came to about $40 million. Since the ship's tactical value in a fluid war with practically no fixed targets was limited, one might be excused for thinking the whole episode was a Navy publicity stunt.

The Navy should have known better, since it has been long at the trade. It even had the first formal military publicity organization—not in the Navy itself, but in the Marine Corps. According to Colonel James A. Donovan, Jr., USMC (Ret.), the Marines set up a public relations office in Chicago in 1907 in an attempt to "outbid the other services for recruits."* Although this was the first formal public relations outfit, the Marines years earlier had a public relations man par excellence—a contemporary of Mahan: John Philip Sousa.

Sousa was the director of the Marine Band from 1890 to 1892 (and of the Navy Band during World War I) and his marches like "Semper Fidelis" and "Stars and Stripes Forever" have stirred the martial spirit in generations of Americans. Ever since Sousa's day, the Navy has made extensive use of musical organizations to woo the public. Navy bands made 600 public appearances last year and a half-dozen other units from the service, ranging from the Navy Steel Band, which produces Caribbean rhythms, to

* *The United States Marine Corps* (New York: Frederick A. Praeger, 1967), p. 181.

the Sea Chanters, a vocal group that wears War of 1812 uniforms, regularly tour the country giving concerts.

The biggest impression the Navy makes on the public, though, is not with Sousa marches or calypso songs but with the display of its warships, from frigate to carrier. As the VIP is impressed at sea, so is the ordinary citizen at dockside.

"Do you have a navigable harbor?" *Direction* asks of the Navy reserve public relations companies among whom it circulates. "How long since a Navy ship visited your port and held an Open House? The potential in good community relations is fantastic." (In FY 68, 770,000 persons participated in Open Houses.)

As noted earlier, the Navy also makes extensive use of top civilian officials of the department and high-ranking officers who travel at taxpayers' expense about the country making speeches. During Fiscal Year 1969 the speakers, whose programs were arranged from Washington, spoke to audiences ranging from the Kiwanis Club of Columbus, Ohio, to the Electronics Industry Association's Government Procurement Relations Department meeting in Key Biscayne, Florida, to a "Freedom Seminar" in San Diego. Forty-two speakers were provided by Washington for "Navy Day" events around the country.

Generally, the topics discussed are strictly Navy, but at times the subject matter can slip into areas of dubious propriety, as will be discussed in a later chapter. Even when the speaker sticks to matters of Navy concern, he can sometimes be carried away by his desire to make the strongest case possible for his service. Something like this apparently happened last year to Admiral Thomas H. Moorer, then Chief of Naval Operations and now Chairman of the Joint Chiefs of Staff.

Speaking to the Veterans of Foreign Wars convention in August 1969, Admiral Moorer expounded on the importance of the aircraft carrier to the nation's world-wide strategic role and on the carrier's strength and relative invulnerability.

"In some fifty wars or near wars since 1946," he told the veterans, "we have not lost a carrier or had one damaged through hostile action."

This strange bit of history caused my colleague from Minnesota, Senator Walter F. Mondale, a critic of the Navy's expanding carrier program, to ask the admiral for a list of the conflicts. Admiral Moorer supplied a list of forty-eight examples, but asked that they be kept classified. Senator Mondale insisted that the information should be public knowledge, and the admiral declassified all but a few. Except for the Korean War and the fighting in Vietnam, the examples were mostly of "alerts" when there had been trouble in one place or another in the world—only a few directly involving the United States. These alerts included the Laos crisis in 1963—in a landlocked country far from the sea; the trouble in 1963 in Jordan, a virtually land-locked country; disorders in Haiti; and riots in Zanzibar.

"To be charitable to the Navy," Senator Mondale observed, "I would say the most embarrassing incidents remained classified."*

The information Senator Mondale got from Admiral

* Wicklein, "The Navy Prepares for World War II," p. 19.

Moorer made a few newspapers, but I would wager that the VFW delegates when they got home more widely spread the story of the "fifty wars" and of the "invulnerability" of our aircraft carriers.

5 | The Army Way

ON THE SECOND PAGE of *The Army Information Officers' Guide* it says:

"Much of the Army's information program is based on the following concept:

"If the Army is good, the story will be good—and public relations will be good. If the Army is bad, the story will be bad and the result bad. In the end, public opinion about the Army reflects what the Army itself is. This is the whole secret of Army public relations."

That is an honest and forthright statement. But after reading the mass of material on Army public relations programs supplied to me by the Chief of Information—and recalling past and present stories of Army activities—I must observe that the "secret of Army public relations" goes much further than letting stories—good and bad—develop on their own. With the money and manpower available in its public relations organization, the Army cannot seem to stay away from self-promotional activities. The ABM Public Relations Program disclosed in the Starbird Memorandum was not a temporary aberration.

Even the Army's own regulations governing information policies show ambiguity between the desire just to inform the public and an equal desire to use information activities as a means of getting public support for Army programs and weapons.

That ambiguity is apparent in the stated objectives of the Army information program as set forth in Army Regulation 360–5:

To keep the public informed concerning the Army and thereby—
    a. Develop public esteem and respect for the Army and Army personnel.
    b. Gain public understanding and support of the Army's role in a sound national military program.
    c. Inspire public confidence in the Army's ability to accomplish its mission now and in the future.

With those goals in mind, it is a short jump from public information to public relations in the promotional sense, and a survey of Army programs shows that they are definitely in that mold.

According to the Chief of Information, the Army in Fiscal Year 1969 employed 612 persons—442 military persons and 170 civilians—in its public affairs program. Eighty-two of these people work for the Office of the Chief of Information in Washington; the others are spread throughout the country and around the world. There are additional hundreds who have public relations functions but are not officially charged to "public information and community relations" activities. *The Army Information Officers' Guide* describes the breadth of these activities:*

"Within the Department of the Army, information organization begins with the Office, Chief of Information, and continues through intermediate headquarters to the post-division and brigade level. At each of these echelons an information staff assists the commander in planning and executing his information program."

The public information activities of the Army, according to the Chief of Information, cost $4.9 million last year—about half of the totals acknowledged by the Air Force and the Navy. Obviously, many of the things the Army does in public relations must be charged to other accounts. For example, the Army informed me that the $4.9 million did not include costs associated with its internal Command Information program—troop indoctrination. Since a portion of this internal information is made available to—and in some cases directed at—the civilian population, these costs in sizeable part should be added to the Army's spending total.**

To illustrate how internal Army Command Information material reaches the general public, let us take the Army's "Big Picture" program. This is a series of thirty-minute films in color, purportedly produced to inform the troops, that annually costs more than $900,000—enough money to produce a respectable series of commercial documentaries.

---

* Later raised in the report to the Senate Appropriations Committee to 1,576 civilian and military employees.

** Later raised in the report to the Senate Appropriations Committte to $13,929,000.

Some fifty-five of these films have been produced in the past two years, and of these seventeen dealt directly with the Vietnam War. It is belaboring the obvious, but they understandably glorify the Army's role in that war.

According to information supplied by the Army, "The Big Picture" is currently being shown to the American public on a regularly scheduled basis by 313 commercial and 53 educational television stations around the country. That is more than half of all television stations in the United States. When you consider that 95 percent of American homes now have television sets, the films' audience must be numbered in the tens of millions.

"The Big Picture" is distributed free to the stations and is used to fill a part of each station's "public affairs" program time required of them by Federal Communications Commission regulations. The Army stresses that the films are supplied only on request, but anyone who has attended a broadcasters' convention has seen promotion material advertising the availability of "The Big Picture" to station owners, people understandably hungry for free material to fill the maw of their program requirements.

As for the Army's claim that the films are primarily intended for Command Information, *The Army Information Officers' Guide* refers to "The Big Picture" as "the Army's official documentary television effort" and urges information officers to be on the alert for local material of "potentially national appeal."

The films are supposed to be documentaries, but along with glorifying the Army they take an approach to the complexities of today's world that is oversimplified and one-dimensional. For example, one "Big Picture" episode titled

"Ready Round the World" is described in the Army's film catalogue as depicting "America's strength in the complex international world of the sixties. It is a film which speaks of men on guard around the world protecting the American way of life." Such a film may be appropriate for showing the soldiers as a part of a training program, but hardly can give the viewing public an objective and considered explanation of our overseas military involvements.

The manner in which this program operates illustrates how the military services can quietly develop their extensive public relations capability with little public knowledge or interference. And the financing of the venture, as already noted, is not even charged to "public information," nor are other extensive film activities the Army uses to influence the public.

All Army audio-visual programs are under the command of the Assistant Chief of Staff for Communications and Electronics with production done by the Signal Corps. Its budget is separate from that for public information. However, Army Regulation 108–5 that lists the types of photographic coverage to be performed by Signal Corps units says, "All types of photographic coverage are used to support the public information program." One of the types of coverage listed is " 'Cold War.' Photographic coverage in support of cold war activities," and the regulation describes the special unit set up to do such coverage. It is the Department of the Army Special Photographic Office (DASPO) "established . . . for the purpose of obtaining filmed documentation of U.S. Army activities in the cold war with primary emphasis on counterinsurgency."

A motion picture team from this Special "Cold War"

71

Photographic Office is on duty in Korea. According to a quarterly report of the Eighth Army Command Information program made late last year, the team shot 32,112 feet of motion picture film and 1,341 still photographs. This included color footage of such things as Republic of Korea Armed Forces Day ceremonies, bridges, roads, and railways throughout Korea, and the "Focus Retina" joint airborne exercises of United States and Korean forces. How much of this production or other "cold war" coverage reached the American public is difficult to estimate, but it can be assumed that some of it did. There were at least 100 Army films made available to the public during Fiscal Year 1969.

The Army is the largest of the services, with more than 45 percent of our men in uniform in its ranks. Practically all men drafted go into the Army. The incidence of casualties among draftees is high, as they now make up about 50 percent of the frontline riflemen in Vietnam. The Army, therefore, is understandably anxious to put itself in the best light possible with the draftees' folks at home. One widely used method is to tell the story of the individual soldier to his parents, his friends, and his fellow townsmen through the Army Home Town News Center located in Kansas City, Missouri.

The center apparently is a kind of journalistic assembly line into which, from Vietnam, Germany, Korea, Thailand, and posts in this country and abroad where American soldiers are stationed, flows the raw material about their promotions, achievements, and activities. Out from Kansas City go the processed news releases, still photographs, television film clips, and radio tapes to an astonishing number of local outlets: 1,700 daily newspapers, 8,300 weeklies, 2,700 radio stations, and 550 television stations.

Though there is no doubt that these stories, pictures, tapes, and films have considerable morale value, they also by their nature—the Army telling its own story—scarcely can be considered objective. The material coming back from Vietnam bears little resemblance to the terrible war as seen in day-to-day reporting of the regular news media.

The Army says that all of its "home town" outlets have requested the material sent to them. Since the home town service in one form or another has been a regular Army activity dating from World War II, "requests" mostly consist of an editor or broadcaster filling in a prepaid return postcard indicating that he wants the Army to continue sending material.

The Army Information Officers' Guide instructs Army men about the form in which the Home Town News Center wants material from the field prepared. It carefully points out, "A statement of the mission and importance of the soldier's unit [should be] worked into the central part of the story." Here is an example of the Center's output, following those instructions. It is caption material for a picture:

CIVIC ACTION

NHA TRANG, VIETNAM (AHTNC)—Big sister is much concerned as baby brother has a head sore examined by Army Specialist Six Richard L. Wallace of El Paso, Texas, in a small village near Nha Trang, Vietnam.

Spc. Wallace, son of Mr. and Mrs. Dean Wallace, 2103 Otillia Drive, Ithaca, N.Y., is a senior medical assistant in the 25th Medical Detachment of the 17th Combat Aviation Group. As a

73

part of the Army's Medical Civic Action Program (MEDCAP), the unit provides medical and dental care for two Vietnamese villages and a Montagnard refugee camp in its area.

Spec. Wallace entered the Army in 1964 and was stationed in Germany prior to arriving in Vietnam last March. He is a graduate of Utica Free Academy and attended Utica College.

The specialist's wife, Shirley, lives at 9316 Vicksburg Drive, El Paso, Texas.

The picture of Specialist Wallace probably went to the *Utica Observer-Dispatch,* the *El Paso Herald-Post* and the *El Paso Times,* and to other publications as well. The Army says that each piece of material produced at the Home Town News Center goes to an average of eight outlets. Much of this output emphasizes non-combat, humanitarian activities such as those in which Specialist Wallace was engaged. As will be noted elsewhere in this book, the military public relations output from Vietnam leans heavily on good works only tangentially connected to the death and destruction of the war itself.

Radio tapes, mostly interviews with individual soldiers but sometimes just greetings to the family and friends, vie with newspaper "home-towners" in the Center's output. Small town radio broadcasting is a highly competitive world, a situation that makes it a fertile field for placing Home Town News Center tapes—particularly around Mother's Day and other holidays with sentimental overtones. Here are excerpts from a few letters received by the Army from radio stations which use the Center's material. All are about tapes originally prepared in Vietnam.

KBJM, Lemmon, S.D.—I think tapes are a great idea. The parents sure did appreciate this Mother's Day greeting and we enjoy cooperating in airing them. We'll be more than happy to put interviews on the air as they are available to us.

WOAY, Oak Hill, W.Va.—"I heard my son on Mother's Day. It's beyond words to express how wonderful it made me feel. Please continue these for other mothers through the years. It's wonderful."

WAZL, Hazleton, Pa.—The parents were very happy, his friends were happy, and so are we. Can use any and all from area in Vietnam. Aired on five different newscasts over two days.

WNEA, Newnan, Ga.—We run these several times a day in our record shows. We've had excellent response from our listeners.

WFAD, Middlebury, Vt.—This is the best public relations the Army has and should be utilized more.

WAYE, Baltimore, Md.—WAYE and Read's Drug Stores sent Mrs. B. a box of candy on Mother's Day. We told her it was on behalf of her son.

In our past wars this kind of activity was known as "bucking up the home front," but this is a different kind of war from those others. The Army's correspondent from Middlebury, Vermont, put his finger on what the tapes are produced for: "public relations." The Army spends more than $500,000 a year on the Home Town News Center and so far as its Vietnam material is concerned it undoubtedly is money spent just as much to make the point that what we are doing there is right and humane as it is to tell "Mom" that her son is well and that the Army is looking out for him.

The military services, and particularly the Army, try to get to "Mom's" boys even while they are in high school. According to the Department of Defense there were 700 Junior Reserve Officer Training Corps units in the country

—teaching military subjects to teen-agers—at the end of Fiscal Year 1969, and it was planned to increase the total to more than 900 by the end of 1970. There were 133,000 high school students in the program last year, a program that cost the taxpayers $10 million.

The value of this expenditure to the country is debatable; its value in purely military terms is, at best, theoretical. The title ROTC has no meaning, for each of the boys who finishes high school after taking the course, even for four years, faces the same routine and period of training when he enlists or is drafted as those who did not bother to shoulder obsolete M-1 rifles in weekly drills.

The purposes of the program, it appears from the ROTC material distributed to high schools, are public relations and military conditioning. The principal theme of this information is directed at adults who may be troubled by the appearance and conduct of today's youth. ROTC, it says, "automatically guarantees the community a well-groomed male student body. . . . The program motivates the young man to be alert and sensitive to the world around him; it motivates him to aspire to greater heights of achievement; it encourages him to play a more active and meaningful citizenship role and to respect properly constituted authority. It develops patriotism and encourages a high sense of personal honor and deportment. Through this program the young man learns first to follow, then to lead, with increasing degrees of responsibility and authority as he progresses."

The idea that public high schools should be a training ground for the armed forces is a dangerous concept, justified neither by national needs nor social policy. The Army —as well as the other armed services—has no business trying to "guarantee the community a well-groomed male

76

student body" in our public schools. And the teaching of good citizenship, respect for authority, and strength of character is the responsibility of parents, our churches, and our schools—not the military, if we wish to remain a democratic society.

Another public relations program carried on by the Army is that of its Exhibits Unit. It spends more than $900,000 a year in the production of models, pictures and display materials that are taken on tours throughout the country. According to one semi-annual report of the Army's Community Relations branch, some 13.5 million persons viewed twenty-two Army exhibits during the last six months of 1968. Another report noted that exhibits during a semi-annual period had been displayed in thirty-four states and more than 1,200 cities. It added:

"A total of 508 minutes of television coverage was received along with well over 3,000 minutes on the radio and more than 4,000 column inches of news coverage in local papers."

Here is a report that any commercial PR man would be happy to show to his client.

At least two of the exhibits are exclusively about Vietnam, and both, like other military PR activities concerning that country, approach the war by indirection. One is a display of "Communist" equipment captured from the Viet Cong and the North Vietnamese. The other, titled "U.S. Army, Vietnam—Building and Defending," is about "the Army's role in Vietnam, a brief outline history of the conflict, and a sampling of the Army's civic action projects to help the people of Vietnam." In the first six months of 1969, this exhibit was shown in Milledgeville, Georgia; Louisville, Kentucky; Altoona, Pennsylvania; Johnstown,

Pennsylvania; Moorestown, New Jersey; Chicago, Illinois; Ripon, Wisconsin; Milwaukee, Wisconsin; Rocky Mount, North Carolina; Wilmington, North Carolina; Montgomery, Alabama; New Orleans, Louisiana; Topeka, Kansas; Overland Park, Kansas; Kansas City, Missouri; Omaha, Nebraska; Fort Dodge, Iowa; Burlington, Iowa, and Hammond, Indiana. During the same period, eleven other Army exhibits were touring 185 cities.

An Army promotional activity that takes up much of the time of commanders and other high ranking officers and demands considerable logistical support is "Community Relations." This program is described in Army Regulation 360–1 as follows:

The broad objective of Army community relations programs is to enhance the effectiveness of the Army by promoting public understanding of the Army mission and by gaining public cooperation with the Army. The programs are designed—
    a. To inform the public on the state of preparedness of the Army.
    b. To develop public understanding and cooperation with the Army, thereby facilitating the accomplishment of the Army mission and objectives.
    c. To promote national security and stimulate patriotic spirit.
    d. To assist recruiting and personnel recruitment.

The regulation lists the kinds of activities the Army should use and sets policies to be followed. The activities include use of aircraft, parachute demonstrations, bands and other musical units, speaking engagements, troop participation in parades and ceremonies, visits of special groups, open houses, and membership for officers in civic and business clubs.

The category of "visits by special groups" was touched on briefly in chapter one—describing the use of the "Operation Understanding" program of the North American Air Defense Command to promote the ABM system. During the period that the Starbird Memorandum had official status, the lists of people participating in this program were heavily weighted with state legislators, city and county officials, and persons of influence from areas where ABM's might possibly be sited. Those being taken on the trips these days are somewhat harder to classify. However, there seems to be a rough common denominator: most come from small towns and cities. Perhaps the Army feels that they may be more impressionable than people from large metropolitan centers. The number of trips made has not diminished since the Starbird incident. In the final six months of Fiscal Year 1969 there were seventeen "Operation Understanding" tours in which 265 persons participated.

Ever since the escalation of the Vietnam War, there has been a parallel escalation in the number of Army speakers appearing before public audiences. The subject of their talks, more often than not, is Vietnam. One of the most active recent speakers has been General William C. Westmoreland, Army Chief of Staff, who between August 7, 1968, and the end of May 1969 made a list of fifty-nine appearances. That is a heavy schedule for a man whose job is running an Army of 1.5 million men.

The lead of their commander has been followed by hundreds of other Army men, for the Army lays great stress on the importance of speeches. *The Army Information Officers' Guide* says, "There is no substitute for personal contact in public relations. . . . The most effective way to tell the Army's story is through the Army's public speaking program."

There apparently is no dearth of uniformed Dale Carnegies. A community relations report at the end of 1967 noted: "All reporting commands indicated an active Army speakers program. . . . The demand for Army speakers on Vietnam has also increased during the period. An estimated 1,000 [sic] speakers per month are scheduled and requested [throughout the country] to speak on Vietnam."

If such demand has continued unabated, this means that on an average night each week no fewer than seven Army speakers appear before public audiences. Those of us who seek to challenge the Administration and concurrently the Army's position on Vietnam can scarcely compete with such an array of speakers. It must be remembered, too, that this is just the Army. The Department of Defense, the Navy, and the Air Force have their speaking programs too. The opportunity to shape the public's mind on Vietnam from the public platform is enormous and disturbing in its implications.

The Army itself has taken official cognizance of the dangers of having military men speak in areas of public controversy. Army Regulation 360–5, which deals with information policy, states:

"In public discussion, all officials of the Department of the Army should avoid discussion of matters which are the responsibility of other Government agencies, i.e., foreign policy is a responsibility of the Department of State."

In Army Regulation 360–1, which deals with community relations, it is stated that "speakers will confine their remarks to discussion of subjects within the cognizance of the Department of Defense." Furthermore, Department of the Army message 703436, "Public Affairs Policy Guidance for Personnel Returning from Vietnam," issued in February

1968, deals specifically with subjects that should or should not be mentioned in public discussion. These include, according to an Army report supplied to me, the specific admonition that "personnel should not speak on the foreign policy implications of the U.S. involvement in Vietnam."

Similar restrictions on the content of speeches have been laid down by the Department of Defense and the other military services. However, as will be seen in chapter eight, many military men interpret the meaning of the restrictions very loosely. Even if the restrictions could be adhered to, the practice of sending military men about the country at taxpayers' expense to "tell the Army story" is a rather unusual way to preserve a democratic society under civilian control.

The preparation of speeches, as anyone who has ever made one knows, is a time-consuming and demanding chore. Officers in the upper echelons of the military can count on the services of their information staffs to produce material for them, but the middle level officers, who make most of the speeches, have no such assistance. The Army has met this need by providing more than twenty different approved canned speeches from which an officer scheduled to speak to some civic, fraternal, or other organization can select his topic.

These packaged materials are known as "Speechmaker Kits" and are prepared by the Command Information Unit. According to the Army, "They are designed for delivery by any Army spokesman to adult military and civilian groups of all kinds." The speeches, of course, are cleared by the Office of the Chief of Information, and consequently are the official words of the United States Army. Here are some

81

of those words from one speech, "The Army—Ready for Any Mission":

... this means the Army must be ready at all times to provide for the security of the nation by supporting our national objectives.

What are these national objectives? First, to prevent the occurrence of total nuclear war or, if it occurs, to make certain that the United States brings it to the most favorable conclusion possible.

Second, to dispel any illusion aggressors may have that they can engage in local military conquests at the expense of the Free World.

And, third, to prevent the Communists from gaining control of independent and new emerging nations through subversion and other covert means, including coercion, reprisals, terrorism, and eventual guerilla warfare.

Another "Speechmaker" talk, formerly known as "Special Warfare" but now bearing the nonviolent title of "The U.S. Role in Stability Operations," says:

The modern U.S. Army is organized and trained to deal with any type of hostility, from the conventional warfare spectrum to all-out nuclear war. Partly as a result of our experience in Vietnam, but mostly because of our analysis of future conflicts, we have determined that limited war will be the most likely form of hostilities to involve the U.S. Army.

This warfare growing out of counterinsurgency—what Mao Tse Tung calls "Peoples' Wars" and Khrushchev called "Wars of Liberation" and "Popular Uprisings." Ruthless enemy insurgents have the advantage over the defense forces of an emerging nation in wars of this type. As we have learned all too clearly in Vietnam, they are also very costly and depend as much, if not more, on psychological and political warfare as well as military combat. *These can be controlled if we are successful in nipping every Communist insurgency in the bud. That is what we hope to do.* [Italics mine.]

This officially cleared speech is available to any Army officer to present to service clubs, fraternal organizations, businessmen's luncheon meetings, veterans groups, and other organizations at a time when we are trying to extricate ourselves from the Vietnam morass. The Army may have learned how to apply new techniques from its Vietnam experience, but apparently it does not recognize the basic mistakes that put us there. It seems almost to be looking for new involvements.

The speech goes on to describe how the Army's Stability Operations would work in another Vietnam:

In one form or another, the host government and its authority will come under internal attack. We call these attackers insurgents. The insurgency may be only expressed discontent or a desire for redress of legitimate grievances, but it is organized and can soon come under the sponsorship of international communism. At the request of the host government, U.S. foreign internal defense policy is brought into play. Working through the recognized government, we attempt to create a climate of law and order. This can mean, and usually does, that we also work on the host government to improve its efficiency, integrity, and ability, while simultaneously developing a sense of dedication to the people, of service to them, and of meeting their needs.

This simplistic approach—with its pat "school solution" —to the problems of countries in turmoil around the world could be shrugged off were it not presented in such deadly earnest and with the *imprimatur* of the Department of the Army. Also, we have acted increasingly in the fashion described. The Dominican Republic adventure, in particular, comes to mind—an unwise and illegal intervention brought about by our mindless reaction to the word "communism." There is no way of telling how many worried American citizens have listened to beribboned brigadier generals, colonels, and others deliver the "Stability Operations" speech* and flash on a screen the slides that accompany it. (One slide shows a globe of the world with a red, slant-eyed octopus sitting in China and encompassing all of Asia in its tentacles.) Whatever the number, they have been given a distorted, oversimplified view of one area of this divided world's problems and a manifestly disproven solution for the ills described.

To the "hard sell" activities in the Army's public relations arsenal should be added the "soft sell" items such as participation of troop formations in parades and local celebrations, parachute jumping demonstrations by the "Golden Knights" team, "open houses" at military installations, and membership of officers in civic clubs in towns near Army bases. These activities are as important to the overall effort as more direct promotional ones—they keep the Army in the public's eye.

There is evidence that the cumulative campaign of the Army has had some effect. In Tacoma, Washington, not too long ago the city's annual Daffodil Festival Parade came at a time when nearby Fort Lewis was celebrating its fiftieth birthday. The parade took as its theme: "Our Heritage—the Military Era."

* According to this speech, the Army has five especially trained groups ready for use anywhere in the world. They are known as Special Action Forces and are based in Okinawa (for Asia), Fort Bragg, North Carolina (for Africa and for the Near East), the Canal Zone (for Latin America), and Germany (for Europe).

6 "Into the Wild Blue Yonder"

EARLY THIS YEAR the Air Force announced that it was giving up its Bagpipe Band as a part of a general economy drive, a laudable action, even though the saving involved was tiny. But the question arises: What was the Air Force doing with a pipe band in the first place? The answer is obvious: It was a public relations gimmick, a part of the huge apparatus the Air Force uses to sell itself to the American public.

I have enough Scots blood in me to thrill to the skirl of "Highland Laddie" or "The Skye Boat Song," but it strikes me as incongruous that a group of American servicemen should be dressed in kilts and sent on tours of the country to polish the image of the United States Air Force at state fairs, high school assemblies, and gatherings of die-hard Gaels.*

* The Royal Air Force has a bagpipe band, appropriately based in Scotland, but it is, I am told, a volunteer organization.

The Bagpipe Band may be missed by some, but the Air Force still has scores of musical organizations available for public performances just about anywhere. These bands, glee clubs, choirs, string quintets, and jazz combos are even used to promote commercial enterprises—just so long as a large crowd is involved. Air Force musical units have participated in half-time entertainment at professional football games. "The Singing Sergeants" have given concerts at Disneyland. The Air Force Academy Band marched in a Macy's Thanksgiving Day Parade.

If you listen to the radio at all, you cannot have failed to have heard "Serenade in Blue," a weekly Air Force Band production. This band and the Air Force Academy Band also make albums of popular music that are distributed free to radio station disc jockeys. It cannot be said that the bands are not kept busy. In one six-month period, musical units from the Air Academy made 486 appearances, which approximates the old three-a-day of vaudeville.

All of this musical activity is pure public relations, something at which the Air Force is expert. From the days of General Billy Mitchell, who demonstrated that battleships could be sunk by air bombardment, through the unification battle of the middle forties, public relations tactics were the hallmark of Air Force attempts to attract attention. Jack Raymond in his book *Power at the Pentagon* tells how a fellow *New York Times* reporter, during the period the Air Force was fighting the Navy for predominance, briefly left his table in the Pentagon restaurant and found on his chair when he returned detailed plans showing how bombers could neutralize and destroy aircraft carriers.

Such vicious inter-service battling is long past, but there

remains rampant rivalry among the services for the public's affection and for their representatives' votes on huge appropriations in Congress. It is more serious than the advertising claims of rival auto manufacturers, and the Air Force is very good at it.

Like all the other services, the Air Force is well aware of the national malaise about warfare and the growing public unhappiness about the size and expense of the armed forces. In an information directive sent in 1968 to all Air Force Commands, then Air Chief of Staff, Gen. J. P. McConnell, said that "in view of current events and notable diverse public views concerning our nation's defense . . ." Air Force "information efforts must make clear that this changing and increasingly complex world demands that our nation's military power be superior, adaptive to change, and capable of rapid application. We must make clear that aerospace power is *uniquely important* in meeting these demands through both its support for the employment of other forces and its own striking power." [Italics mine.] Generals on down the line were instructed to "promote awareness, understanding, and appreciation" of the fact that "clearly superior United States aerospace forces capable of defeating the enemy offer the surest means of deterring global war." Countering the "aerospace threat to our security," the directive stated, can only be done through "maintaining superiority" in our own forces. Sufficiency may be enough for President Nixon but it is not enough for the Air Force.

In promoting its public affairs objectives during Fiscal Year 1969, the Air Force reported to me that it had spent $9,424,000 and used the services of a full-time staff of 904 persons. In the Pentagon alone, there were 105 full-time people—55 officers, 9 enlisted men, and 41 civilians—manning a public relations operation that costs $1,600,000 annually. The rest of the 904 were spread through offices in New York, Chicago, and Los Angeles, and at the 122 Air Force bases and major installations around the country. Additional thousands have public functions collateral to other duties. Recently the city offices have been closed for economy reasons.*

Among the mail I received after my December 1969 speeches in the Senate on Defense Department public relations programs was a letter from a former airman whose service tour included being a full-time public relations man at Lackland Air Force Base in Texas. Conceding that there may be overstatement in the letter stemming from the man's obvious unhappiness about the kind of a military job he had to perform, it is still worth quoting:

Most Americans are unaware that they are the target of a ceaseless propaganda campaign waged by the largest advertising agency in the world. We know of course that generals and other Pentagon officials engage in political activities, such as speaking before pro-war groups. But we do not realize that the U.S. military maintains an active, professional advertising department ("information office") on every one of its thousands of installations around the world.

For two and one-half years of my recent term in the U.S. Air Force, I was assigned to one such "information" office. . . . Our mission was identical to that of any commercial advertising agency: to "push" our product (the Air Force) as hard as we could—to capitalize on its successes and to conceal its blunders, creating a favorable public image of the Air Force.

The information office had a lavish budget and a large staff

* In the report to the Senate Appropriations Committee these figures were raised to $12,390,000 and 1,305 full-time employees for FY 1969.

(25 persons including well-paid civilian employees, NCO's, and officers through the rank of colonel). All day, every day our primary business was grinding out "news" stories and features for daily and weekly newspapers, magazines, radio, and television. We also were active in other forms of public relations techniques such as taking visiting congressmen and civic officials on "canned" tours of the base. The local news media were receptive to our efforts, which consisted largely of glorifying the Air Force role in Vietnam.

This young man's letter touched on only a few of the dozens of activities the Air Force carries on to influence public opinion.

Like any good advertising agency, the Air Force Office of Information has an Information Development Branch that "develops short and long range story ideas and places them with all types of communications media." In other words, the Office of Information does not wait for events to happen, but looks at all aspects of the product it has to sell for things that will catch public attention. The Information Development Branch also thinks up media production ideas like a weekly TV film program that goes to 450 commercial stations. And "Pro Sports Report," a five-minute radio program that carries "Air Force promotional spot announcements" and is sent to 150 "major market commercial radio stations." Considering the flood of sports programs that fill the airwaves, it would seem to me that the Air Force product is redundant, but apparently it is used.

Another section of the Office of Information, the Special Projects Branch, "conducts the Air Force books and magazine features program. It maintains the Air Force story book and recommends marketing procedures for these themes and performs liaison with industry concerning public information programs of mutual interest." "Marketing procedures?" Use of the terminology of Madison Avenue appears somewhat unseemly for a military organization, but then it could be that the young man who served at Lackland was right in his "advertising agency" analogy. Beyond the terminology, however, is the explicit statement that the branch works with the arms industry on public relations activities "of mutual interest." I have no idea of the extent of this cooperation, but considering the hand-in-glove relationship between the Air Force and its suppliers, the connection gives a new dimension to the size of the PR program.

The Air Force uses radio, television, and motion pictures much as the Army does. Along with weekly film clips for TV and the radio "Pro Sports Report" already mentioned, 4,000 radio stations—nearly two-thirds of all of the AM and FM outlets in the country—carry the weekly musical program "Serenade in Blue." A taped features program for use three times a week is sent to 1,139 radio stations. And a thirty-minute Christmas TV show each year is sent to 204 stations.

It is hard to put one's finger on the cost of the Air Force's film production for public consumption. All Air Force films are produced by the Aerospace Audio-Visual Service, whose budget of $10.9 million is buried among the funds of the Military Air Transport Command and seems to be used mostly for training, recruiting, and technical films. However, 24 of its 148 motion pictures and all 36 of its TV film clips produced in Fiscal Year 1968 were released for public use.

One of the films produced during the period concerns a rather unusual American relationship—our military bonds with Franco's Spain. The film, *Exercise Pathfinder Express,* shows Spanish and American forces fighting against a hypothetical foe curiously labeled "Aggressor Republic." It was a joint exercise that followed a scenario—unknown to our State Department—which called for U.S. troops to parachute in to help Spaniards fight insurgents.

According to the Air Force films catalogue, the movie "depicts the largest airborne training exercise in Europe." Six thousand men were involved, and transport planes were flown from as far away as Tennessee to participate.

The ground phase of the exercise was held near Zaragoza —old Saragossa, seat of the ancient kingdom of Aragon and not far from the Ebro River battlefield where Franco forces and Loyalists fought a bloody and decisive battle for nearly four months in late 1938. I'm sure there are still people of Loyalist sympathies living in the vicinity who wondered what American troops were doing fighting by the side of Franco's. The Air Force noted no anomaly. As the film's narrator says, "The extremely successful test also demonstrated the ability of Spanish and American forces to work closely in a realistic combat situation."

The narrator goes on to say, "The operation was brought to a close with a traditional parade, as forces from both countries marched proudly before their commanders." Generalissimo Franco was not in the reviewing stand, but his "personal deputy," Captain-General Augustino Munoz-Grandes, Vice President, watched a part of the maneuvers with our then Ambassador, Angier Biddle Duke.

After the parade, there are shots of Spanish and American troops watching a bullfight, then the fadeout—a panoramic view of a pastoral scene outside of Zaragoza. The

91

commentator says: "There is no doubt that *Exercise Pathfinder Express* demonstrated that if the stillness of the European countryside is ever broken by the battle tread of an aggressor, United States forces, combined with those of our Allies, will be ready."

Perhaps the Air Force is privy to something that I have not yet been told, for I am unaware of any treaty, agreement, or other arrangement we have with Spain that obligates the United States to go to her defense.

Another surprising Air Force "public release" film is titled *The Other Side of the World*. It "documents civic action programs conducted in Thailand's rural areas by the Air Force's 606th Air Commando Squadron. Shows operation of medical and dental clinics and construction of sanitation facilities. Also depicts educational programs for children."

Until I saw this listing in the Air Force film catalogue, I had not realized that our airmen in Thailand in the late 1960s were engaged in pacification programs. I have since learned that the program was halted, but I often wonder if my committee might learn more about American commitments around the world by watching Defense Department movies than from briefings by officials of the Executive branch.

For years, Air Force units have been criss-crossing the country with impressive and expensive exhibits and exhibition flights by the USAF precision flying team, the Thunderbirds. The exhibits were shown at twenty-three state fairs during the late summer and early fall of 1969. Showings of exhibits were not restricted to state fairs, but were put on at scores of county and regional fairs as well and in many of the new shopping malls that surround our cities. In all, the exhibits were shown in 136 places between August 1 and September 20, 1969. During the same period the spectacular Thunderbirds put on their act twenty-eight different times.

The Air Force makes sure that it is noticed.

Like the other services, the Air Force maintains an active speakers bureau, and each month Washington sends to all commands a bulletin of coming speaking engagements and appearances of top-level Air Force officials. On an average, these bulletins list more than 100 engagements a month. But these are only a small part of Air Force-wide speaking activity, for all officers are encouraged to seek platforms from which to tell the Air Force story. A semi-annual Community Relations report of the Air University, Maxwell Air Force Base, Alabama, says: "Air University personnel made 1,574 speeches, radio broadcasts and television appearances. Live audiences totaled almost 135,000, while television appearances and radio broadcasts expanded the total audience to well into the millions. Lt. Gen. A. P. Clark, the Air University Commander, spoke on 23 different occasions."

The Air University apparently misses no opportunity in its attempts to influence people. Another report tells of its Dean of Curriculum conducting training seminars for forty United Givers Fund executives. He also made the "kickoff" speeches for the fund raising campaigns in six cities, three of them as far away as North Dakota.

As might be expected with all of the planes at its disposal, the Air Force has an even more elaborate "distinguished visitors" program than the Army. And it flies its clients to more interesting places—like Las Vegas,

93

Hawaii, Florida, and Europe. These junkets take various forms. Some are for people from the areas surrounding air bases and are designed to "improve community relations." Others are blatant in their purpose—to sell expensive and controversial Air Force projects like the C-5A to "opinion-molders." Others take newsmen to places their papers or stations ordinarily would not send them to cover "stories" of benefit to the Air Force. Others are just back-scratching tours for people the Air Force wants to influence. For example, 100 teachers attending something called an "Aerospace Workshop" at Middle Tennessee University, Murfreesboro, were flown to Dayton, Ohio, and back to Tennessee. The official report of the trip says. "As a public affairs function this airlift accomplished a two-fold purpose. It gave us an opportunity to 'show and tell' the teachers about Sewart's [Sewart Air Force Base] tactical/airlift mission. . . . It also gave the teachers an opportunity to visit Wright-Patterson AFB and the USAF Museum."

The Community Relations reports frequently are quite bald in their descriptions of the "public affairs purpose" accomplished. Nineteen men from the Oklahoma City area, "who serve on various community programs beneficial to the Air Force," were taken to Kelly AFB near San Antonio, Texas, for an overnight stay. "This trip provided [them] with an insight into the operations of another AFLC [Air Force Logistic Command] operation and of the San Antonio Air Materiel Area's civic promotion activities," the report says.

Thirty-six men from Big Springs, Texas, and surrounding area "who work in cooperation with Webb AFB," in April 1969 were flown to Eglin Air Force Base, Florida, for a pleasant two days of spring sunshine and "were given a broader view of Air Force functions." A year earlier nineteen other Big Springs men were flown to Florida "to further cement good relations."

The junketing list is a long one. Here are a few other examples:

1. A trip by a group of Texas attorneys to Wright-Patterson Air Force Base at Dayton to "give prominent members of the civilian bar throughout the State of Texas" an opportunity "to become familiar with the Air Force's history and mission."

2. A three-day tour of Loughlin Air Force Base in Texas by officials from small cities near Scott Air Force Base in Illinois for "orientation."

3. A flight to Illinois from California, with an overnight stop in Las Vegas, for thirty-six members of Chambers of Commerce in three small cities near Travis Air Force Base, California.

The Air Force's wooing of the press is interesting to examine. A few good newspapers will accept military travel only when it is the sole means of getting a story. However, many papers and radio and television stations eagerly accept free trips that are then parceled out as "rewards" to editors and reporters. The Air Force trip reports stress the "impact" of the press junkets. For example, at the end of 1968, twenty newsmen, most of them from weekly papers in the Kansas City area, were flown to Cape Kennedy "to build rapport and improve media relationships between this headquarters and the greater Kansas City news media." To give eleven newsmen from Oregon "familiarization with the reserve associate program in three major markets," they were flown to Hawaii on a two-day trip. Eight California newspaper, radio, and TV reporters were flown from the West Coast to Nurenberg, Germany, in early 1969, to see an Air Force training exercise. En route five people were picked up in St. Louis and a weekly editor picked up in South Carolina. Some of the official reports of this trip made to the Air Force Office of Information in Washington were glowing:

Outstanding feature story and picture coverage in the *St. Louis Globe-Democrat.*

Well read story and picture coverage in the *Walterboro Press and Standard,* Walterboro, S.C.

Very good radio and TV coverage in St. Louis area.

These people who were flown to Germany got, in effect, a free tour of Europe, for their orders read "Variations in itinerary are authorized." That means they didn't have to turn around and come home when the exercise was finished, but could pick up passage on any of the many Air Force planes that routinely fly from Europe to the United States "on a space available basis."

None of the cold facts above give an indication of the enormous amount of time and effort the Air Force expends on the people it takes on the various junkets it sets up. However, among the material supplied to me by the Air Force on its public relations activities was an "After Action" report written by an Information Officer who accompanied the editor of a small California weekly newspaper on an eight-day trip to Japan. I must have gotten the report by inadvertence, for it is quite revealing of the careful and considerate care with which civilians are treated.

The editor accompanied an Air Force Reserve crew on

a training flight from California north to Washington, thence on to Hawaii, Wake Island, Japan, and back through Iwo Jima, Wake Island, Hawaii and home.

The "After Action" report says:

Mr. T. was met and briefed by local IO's at McChord AFB [Washington], Wake Island Air Station, and Tachikawa Air Base [Japan]. Mr. T. was very impressed by the professional support given to him . . .

Due to the change of itinerary, the unexpected landing at Iwo Jima was a delightful treat for Mr. T. He was a naval officer during World War II and was stationed in a destroyer during the Iwo Jima conflict. The U.S. Coast Guard personnel stationed there drove Mr. T. and the reserve crew from the Japanese air base to their station. . . . The Commander of the Japanese base who was an ex-Kamikaze pilot and his personnel were also very courteous and hospitable.

This Information Officer feels that the mission was an unqualified success. . . . During these days, more close contact with the news media such as this and allowing them to become a part of various missions as a firsthand witness would certainly make them realize that the U.S. Air Force and AFRes [Air Force Reserves] are their own organizations and they are here to serve the public.

Multiply the attention given to this one weekly editor by several thousand and you can get some idea of the time and money spent by the Air Force with only one of its techniques for wooing public opinion.

During a six-month period before Senator William Proxmire's House-Senate Committee on Economy in Government began hearings on cost "overruns" of astronomically expensive Air Force projects, but while his staff was conducting preliminary investigations, the Air Force shuttled at least seven groups to "aerospace industries" to show them what was going on. Three groups were taken to the Lockheed plant in Marietta, Georgia, where the C-5A is assembled. They came from Utah, from Congressman Rivers' own Charleston, South Carolina, and from Texas and Oklahoma—a total of 110 persons. A group from Sacramento, California, and a dozen newsmen from the Chicago area, were flown to Forth Worth, Texas, where General Dynamics makes the controversial F-111. The newsmen were taken there to see the transfer of some of these aircraft to the Australian Government. The final two groups, one a group of newsmen from Ohio and the other the "Dayton Presidents Club," also from Ohio, were taken on separate trips to North American–Rockwell, missile manufacturers in Los Angeles.

The examples of Air Force promotional travel I have described are only a small part of the overall effort. Each command seems to have its own junkets. The Strategic Air Command Headquarters in Nebraska, in its "Community Relations" report, lists five groups of "distinguished visitors" it entertained—from Boston, Minneapolis–St. Paul, New York City, Los Angeles, and San Antonio—and twelve "specialized groups," ranging from the Smaller Business Association of New England to "New York Artists." These groups totaled 662 persons—in a period of six months. The Aerospace Defense Command in Colorado reported that its distinguished visitors program brings eighteen to twenty groups to its installations annually from various parts of the country to "expose 450–500 key community leaders . . . to aerospace defense."

A sentence that appears in most of the official orders setting up these tours is "Travel is necessary in the public service." Just what "public service" is involved is beyond my ken, but the travel certainly is at the public expense. The junketeers are flown about the country in a variety of transport planes ranging from huge turbo-prop C-130s to comfortable "commanders aircraft." The costs are enormous. According to the Air Force, it costs $14.9 million a year to fly and support a squadron of sixteen C-130s, or more than $900,000 per plane. None of these transportation costs, of course, are included in the $9.4 million the Air Force says it spends on public relations activities.

The Air Force has 122 major installations spread around the country. Creating local empathy for their presence is a big job, what with the noise of low flying jets, "sonic booms," the demands put on local housing, schools, and municipal services. Consequently, "community relations," in the sense of trying to make the best of a sometimes difficult situation, are assiduously cultivated. But the Air Force carries its "community relations" activities far beyond mere mollification of local complaints and easing of problems. The extent of base community relations activities seems to be limited only by the imagination and energy of the base commander and information officer.

Two of the more energetic and imaginative, it is apparent from reports I have received, are at the Air Defense Weapons Center at Tyndall Air Force Base, Florida. The Center information office produces a daily column for the newspaper published in nearby Panama City, stages four radio shows a week on the local radio station, and one television show. "Community civic leaders" are invited to a dove shoot on the base each fall, and the Air Force property is open to all during the hunting season. An annual event is

"Civilian Law Enforcement Day," with police and other law enforcement officers invited to lunch with the commander and then taken on a tour of the base.

Even Air Force chaplains have a role in selling their service. Strategic Air Command reports that chaplains from Whiteman Air Force Base frequently are guest preachers in churches at nearby Knob Noster, Missouri, contribute devotional editorials to the local weekly newspaper, deliver sermons on the radio, and provide "invocations, benedictions, and on occasion act as guest speakers" at the Parent-Teacher Association. Down in Mississippi at Keesler Air Force Base, chaplains in one six-month period "participated in 22 charitable programs, sponsored nine cultural-educational activities, conducted 30 religious services in the civilian community, and participated in 105 radio and television programs." All of these activities are undoubtedly laudable, but is it the role of the Air Force to provide them?

The Alaska Air Command report is particularly revealing. It says: "Because the Air Force population is such a great part of the state population, any public event in some way involves the Air Force. Exhibits, band engagements, appearances by Air Force commanders, motion pictures, slides, speakers, etc. are supplied on request for the public throughout the state. Nine of the 23 remote stations are so remote they don't even have a native village in their immediate area, but the others all participate in community activities to some degree. From the Aleutian Chain to the north coast, Alaskans have learned that being near an Air Force installation is beneficial."

The Air Force is not averse to pointing out just how

beneficial its presence can be. The Special Weapons Center at Kirtland Air Force Base near Albuquerque, New Mexico, invited that city's Chamber of Commerce to a breakfast on the base at which the Center's commander "presented Kirtland's first annual report."

"The event set a precedent," says the Tactical Air Force's semi-annual community relations report, "emphasizing Kirtland's economic impact on the city as well as the state. Out of a $33 million base research and development budget, $11 million was expended in the Albuquerque area."

There is, of course, nothing sinister about all of these "community relations" activities. Nor is the rest of the huckstering the Air Force carries on itself meretricious. I am, however, deeply bothered by its goal—persuading the American people of the special importance of the Air Force in our society and of its need for more and more and more of the country's resources. This goal the Air Force up to now has certainly achieved. Measured in dollars, its public relations program must be termed a resounding success in obtaining and spending the taxes of the citizens of this country.

7 | Twisted Images

MILITARY PUBLIC RELATIONS men spend a very large amount of time, thought, and the taxpayers' money on making films of one kind and another. From their point of view, there is good reason for interest in the television tube and motion pictures.

The war in Vietnam has been the most assiduously reported conflict in history, but because of the unorthodox nature of the fighting, press and television coverage has lacked clear definition and climactic moments. A war fought in hamlets and jungle against a largely unidentifiable enemy capable of shifting his points of attack and defense produces no flag-raisings of the Iwo Jima sort. Instead, there has been an unending daily trail of blood and death and destruction which modern communications has brought nightly on television into American homes.

We all remember too many dreadful evening television scenes: a young Marine setting fire to the palm-frond roof of a shack with his cigarette lighter; piles of very young, very dead bodies atop an armored personnel carrier returning from battle; ballooning napalm; defoliated forests. Such coverage has caused many military men to complain that not enough attention has been given to the positive side of our involvement.

To show the positive side, the Department of Defense itself since 1966 has been in the television news business in Vietnam, producing what it calls "V-Series" films for use by commercial stations in the United States. It has five camera crews working out of Saigon—a number I am told equal to that of one major network in Vietnam and larger than the other two—charged with covering "feature aspects of the military participation in Southeast Asia." These "feature aspects," the Assistant Secretary of Defense for Public Affairs, Daniel Henkin, wrote me, "are often ignored or bypassed by the national news media because of the pressure of hard news events. [The teams] are not in competition with civilian news media. Rather they supplement the coverage of the major networks. The high usage of the material produced by these teams is indicative of their efforts."

Defense also might have added that the teams' production is high—at least several rough cut film stories a week are shipped by air from Saigon to Washington. They are processed by United Press International Telenews, screened at the Pentagon and cleared for free distribution by the networks and other television news organizations.

Since the entire "V-Series" undertaking was aimed at propagandizing the American people in support of past and present Administration Vietnam policy, it came as no great shock to me when I learned that some films were "staged." It was almost inevitable that fakery would be needed to portray war scenes that guaranteed that the Administration's efforts would be put in the best light.

An Air Force sergeant, with sixteen years in military filmmaking, and two years in Vietnam, told of how he participated in staging three films designed to make the South Vietnamese forces look good. In one instance, an AC-47 gunship—which normally provided support at night to various fire support bases—was flown over a free-fire zone off the coast just for the benefit of the military film crew. According to the sergeant, the specially planned photographic flight lasted four hours while the AC-47 shot into the water knowing full well that there was no enemy below.

When the film was edited and released in 1969 it bore the title, *South Vietnam's Fire Dragons Rule the Night Skies,* and nowhere did it indicate that the film was staged rather than actual combat.

In another instance, the sergeant described a film shot at a fire support base jointly operated by Vietnamese and American troops. During the period of time the film crew was at the fire base, there was one particular engagement where the crew was with an American group which got into action and they filmed that action. However, since the desire was to show the Vietnamese, the day after the real action a company of Vietnamese troops from the fire support base were put on support craft, went down the river to a nondescript spot and staged a landing with the Vietnamese infantry disembarking from the boats and running through the rice paddies as if the enemy were all around. When the crew had enough film, the Vietnamese got back on their boats and returned to the base. The footage of authentic combat action was not used, and according to our source, the released film was centered around the staged river boat landing of Vietnamese forces.

A review of the titles released between October and December 1969 shows how the stress was put on promoting Vietnamization. Fourteen of thirty newsfilms released featured Vietnamese activities or combined United States–Vietnamese efforts. Among them were: *South Vietnamese Forces Guard Island in Siam Gulf Against Viet Cong, South Vietnamese Fighter Pilots Fly F-5 "Freedom Fighter," U.S. and Vietnamese Troops Move in with Villagers to Keep Hamlet Free, "Vietnamization" of River Patrol Boats Moving Ahead Rapidly, Republic of Vietnam Aircraft Mechanics Whiz Through Aircraft Conversions, Allied Troops Cooperate to Stop Communist Infiltration into South Vietnam, The Republic of Vietnam's Air Force Demonstrates Ground Support Ability, South Vietnamese Navy Receives Coast Guard Cutters in "Operation Scatter," Navy Turns Over Eighty River Boats to South Vietnamese.*

Some $400,000 is spent supporting the five camera crews and the contract work done in the United States to edit the film into usable television material. I doubt if any other department of government could afford—or be authorized —to spend this kind of money for what is clearly a propaganda effort.

Vice President Agnew may believe that network commentators have a monopoly on news presentation to the country, but the fact is that local stations also produce their own news shows, and there are few of any consequence that do not have at least a half-hour of such pro-

106

gramming each day. Because local news directors often find it difficult to put together enough visual material to fill the program time alloted to them, they welcome the "V-Films."

When I inquired of the Department of Defense about these films, Assistant Secretary Henkin, replied:

"We feel that services for the electronic journalism media, such as the V-Series releases, are similar to printed releases by which we seek to serve the needs of the printed journalism media. We have therefore undertaken to provide similar services for both the electronic and printed media while recognizing that their technical needs are different."

The answer seems to me to be considerably less than logical for it does not take into account the vast differences in the editorial workings of the two media. The newspaper can rewrite the press release, expand on it with information obtained at its own initiative, shorten it and bury it among the want-ads, or throw it in the wastebasket. The television editor can use the film or discard it but when it is used, it is seen and heard by every viewer. Everything on television is on "Page One."

Reporting the news visually is a most delicate process and one that television has not yet mastered. Some of the recent criticism of the medium has not been without justification, and the good people on television recognize the need for constant vigilance against "over-exposure" and bias. It is hard to understand why they have so readily accepted the military's using their medium to sell the American people on the Vietnam war policy.

In his letter, Mr. Henkin stated that Defense had the

authority to make the "V-Series" films under a directive that says the department's public affairs program will "provide the American people with maximum information about the Department of Defense consistent with national security." This policy has been stretched far beyond its stated limits. These days, the "V-Series" is heavily involved with publicizing the South Vietnamese. Until the Vietnamization program began, the ratio of films picturing the South Vietnamese and our "allies" was about one in five. Since then, approximately half of the films produced have been in support of this theme.

Here are some excerpts from scripts of films made since Vietnamization began:

SOUTH VIETNAMESE FIGHTER PILOTS FLY F-5 "FREEDOM FIGHTER"

Vietnam Air Force fighter pilots flying the supersonic F-5 "Freedom Fighter" have been taking on more varied combat roles in operations against the Viet Cong and North Vietnamese Army troops as part of the growing Vietnamization program taking place in all branches of the Republic of Vietnam military. . . . Many of these pilots have logged 2,000 to 3,000 hours of combat in the F-5 and, in the process, have earned the respect of pilots everywhere for their prowess with the supersonic aircraft.

SOUTH VIETNAM'S "FIRE DRAGONS" RULE NIGHT SKIES

The South Vietnamese Air Force has taken over the night flying combat mission of the AC-47 "Fire Dragons" from American aircrews in the III and IV Corps areas and compiled an enviable record against enemy infiltrators. . . . The planes cover about one-third of the land of South Vietnam and have been highly effective in helping ground forces defend outposts.

REPUBLIC OF VIETNAM AIRCRAFT MECHANICS
WHIZ THROUGH AIRCRAFT CONVERSIONS

Vietnamese Air Force mechanics stationed at Binh Thuy Air
Base in South Vietnam's delta region recently whizzed through a
[six-month] change-over course in helicopter and attack aircraft.
. . . The hard-working officers and men of the VNAF 74th Technical Group completed their training well ahead of schedule.

To carry the illustration farther, consider a few repre-
sentative titles of other films: *Former Viet Cong Families
Establish New Hamlet in South Viet Nam, New Rice Pro-
viding Better Life for South Vietnamese Refugees,* and
*South Vietnamese Volunteers Receive Popular Forces
Training.*

In December 1969, I had a letter from a sergeant in
charge of one of the "V-Series" crews. Here is an excerpt
from that letter, written after I had made my speeches in
the Senate criticizing the Pentagon's propaganda machine:

"Although I may not wholly agree with your remarks,
there is much validity in what you have said and it is a
constant battle for myself to try to change the style of the
story we are providing. Our job here could have a far
reaching effect on the population of the U.S. if we were
allowed to film the stories that should be filmed and after
filming these stories the power to be in the Pentagon would
allow such stories to be released.

"To give you specific instances with regard to propagandizing the war, about four months ago while filming
various jobs we were advised to concentrate on the Vietnamese doing various jobs. Although I will readily admit
that some Vietnamese are doing more, we are filming so
much of the Vietnamese and what they are doing that it

certainly would appear from looking at our stories that the Vietnamese have taken a major share of the war as their own. This however is not the case, at least in my humble opinion. We are just showing them more, thereby making it look as though they are really working faster. . . . I am enclosing release sheets of the stories I have worked on while on this job and I feel that you will readily see that the jobs are not very closely related to the actual conditions that presently exist in this country."

This was not a letter from an uphappy draftee, but from a sixteen-year veteran of the Air Force on his second tour in Vietnam who just wanted to keep on making films, but films "about the combat role of the U.S. soldier in Vietnam."

"The actual conditions that presently exist" in Vietnam trouble many of us who have doubts about the effectiveness of Vietnamization; and the propaganda efforts of the Administration, through the Department of Defense, do not ease these doubts a bit. Of all the examples of military propaganda and public relations effort that I have examined, the "V-Series" films are the most blatant. The pre-planned promotion of Vietnamization shows the weakness of the whole program. But what is worse, this presentation as balanced and objective reporting surely lies far outside the proper bounds of legitimate government information activity.

The Department of Defense likes to dabble in film-making. Besides propagandizing the American people with television films produced expressly to show the positive side of the war in Vietnam, the military to a considerable degree also ensures that the presentation of military themes in commercial motion pictures and documentaries "will benefit the DoD or otherwise be in the national interest."

The quoted phrase is from Department of Defense Instruction 5410.15, "Delineation of DoD Audio-Visual Public Affairs Responsibilities and Policies," a document that gives the requirements a commercial film producer must meet to get assistance from the military for his production. At first glance, these requirements seem sensible enough. When you consider some of the scenes purported to represent men of the armed services in action, in camp, and on the town that have been shown in motion pictures and on television over the years, to ask for "authenticity of the portrayal of military operations or historical incidents, persons, or places" does not seem to be asking too much. Nor do other requirements set forth in the instruction seem unwarranted. These include "compliance with accepted standards of dignity and propriety," noninterference with the "operational readiness" of the military services, restriction of filming to "normal military activities" to the largest extent possible, and payment to the government for the use of military equipment and facilities.

However, another document, Instruction 5410.16, which spells out the procedures that must be followed by a producer who wants military assistance, when added to by the Department of Defense's use of these procedures, results in something resembling censorship.

To make any film, whether it be a feature motion picture or a television documentary that largely depends for its dramatic effect on factual authenticity of military scenes, the cooperation of the armed services is practically a *sine qua non.* In the archives of the Department of Defense are millions of feet of film shot in combat or in training—dramatic footage of planes, weapons, warships, and men in action. From the Pentagon's archives the producer can purchase at low cost appropriate footage to give reality to dramatic incident or to tell a documentary story. Also, the military services have the equipment and personnel that can be photographed in the kind of action or scene a script may require.

But before a producer can obtain the assistance he needs from the military to make his film, his project is subject to a process of review by the Office of the Assistant Secretary for Public Affairs that in effect makes the Department of Defense an overseer of the production. The producer first must submit in writing to the Assistant Secretary for Public Affairs his proposal for a motion picture or television documentary "stating the story objectives of the project and the identifiable benefits for the DoD, and agreeing to abide by the provisions" of pertinent regulations. The Assistant Secretary's office then gives its reaction to the project and, if asked, will "give guidance, suggestions, and access for technical research in the producer's endeavor to prepare a script which might qualify the project ultimately for assistance." If assistance is desired, four copies of the film's script must be submitted for "evaluation and review," and an itemized list of the kinds of assistance needed from the military must be provided. Only after the script is approved are arrangements made to provide shooting assistance. This can range from the sale of reels of action film to making a submarine available—as was done for nine days in the making of *Ice Station Zebra,* starring Rock Hudson—or to turning over a sizeable part of a military installation to the filmmaker—as was done for John Wayne's *The Green Berets.*

Except for a rare request from a television producer for military assistance in making an episode for a series, television film projects approved by the Department of Defense for assistance are of a news or purely informational nature. "If a documentary program represents an effort by a legitimate producer or network," the Pentagon has informed me, "if it is intended to inform the public objectively; if it does not compromise national security; if the subject involves only unclassified areas, activities, and information; if the assistance can be offered without interference to a mission or additional cost to the Government; and if it is not contrary to the best interest of the Department of Defense and the Government, a request for military participation will very likely be honored."

A television script, like the moviemaker's, has to be approved beforehand and the finished product presented for review—a process that may inhibit any kind of penetrating examination of possibly improper activity or errant behavior. A sizeable number of requests from television producers do not meet the military criteria. Over a five-year period, the proportion of "turn downs" received by television producers—218 proposals, 30 rejections—was approximately the same as those for motion pictures. Some of the TV rejections were made for plausible enough reasons—unavailibility of high-ranking officials on desired filming dates, operational conditions, or the inadvisability of discussing unresolved questions of policy in front of the camera. But most of the rejections, statedly made for se-

113

curity reasons, were of proposals concerning matters of great public moment—chemical and biological warfare, antiballistic missiles, and aspects of the Vietnam fighting.

If the Defense Department believes a commercial film script is in its "best interests," as Instruction 5410.16 puts it, a project officer may be assigned to work with the producing company. His role is much more than that of a technical adviser. He is on hand to "assure that the production adheres to the approved script and approved list of assistance requirements," to "attend pertinent production conferences," and to "suspend assistance when action by the producing company is contrary to stipulations governing the project and to the best interest of DoD . . ."

When shooting is finished and the film put together, the filmmaker is then required to submit the completed production to the Assistant Secretary for Public Affairs for an official review, "preferably before the interlock stage" (i.e., before the action and sound are finally put together), so that changes can be made if necessary. This review ostensibly is to ensure accuracy and check for violations of security.

Even if a filmmaker does not require physical assistance and the Department of Defense involvement entails only the sale of stock footage, the review process is supposed to be followed. The military is quite firm on the subject. Among material I received from Defense when I inquired about assistance given to commercial filmmakers was a brief summary titled "General Information: Motion Picture Film Production." It said in part:

There are no requirements for any company to come to the Department of Defense for assistance or even to submit its project for comment. Informational assistance, such as furnishing tech-

114

nical or historical facts, is given to any producer or writer regardless of the story. Likewise, in keeping with the Freedom of Information Act, stock footage is authorized for sale for research and study purposes regardless of the story content. The use of such stock footage, however, in any commercial motion picture is considered a form of assistance and before the sale of footage is authorized established criteria and policies are followed.

During the past five years, the Department of Defense says it has authorized assistance to the producers of forty-three feature motion pictures; in this same period, it refused assistance to eight others. The reasons for these "turn downs" range from "an uncomplimentary portrayal" of the President to lack of "positive value." "Embarrassment" might have been cited as the reason for two rejections. One was a film titled *Palomares Incident*, the story of which was based on the loss of a hydrogen bomb in the Mediterranean after the collision of a bomber and an aerial tanker over Spain in 1966. "No positive value seemed to be inherent in dramatizing and publicizing worldwide such accidents," was the comment made by Defense. The second film, submitted last year, was titled *The Weapon*. Defense comment on this was: "This story was about a USAF aircraft carrying a nuclear bomb which was forced to land in the Middle East where Israeli and Jordanian forces try to retrieve the bomb for their national use. Assistance was turned down because a story about accidents involving nuclear weapons is not in the best national interest . . ."

Plausible and undoubtedly possible dramatic content can be a reason for a "turn down." Such a decision was made concerning a film titled *The Gunner* about a psychopathic Air Force gunner. "The story," the Defense comment said, "in the opinion of the Air Force would not serve any useful

115

purpose for that service and any consideration of assistance should be considered unfavorably." Sequences in *Remagen Bridge,* a World War II story, that showed an officer "condoning" a soldier's robbing dead Germans and an officer threatening another with a pistol and an enlisted man knocking an officer into a bomb crater were among the reasons for another "turn down."

Among the forty-three films that qualified for assistance was the sexy James Bond fantasy *Goldfinger,* in which the gold reserves at Fort Knox are stolen. For this, the Department of Defense "authorized filming of scheduled training exercises where small aircraft dropped simulated gas on troops; scenes of entrance of Fort Knox, Kentucky, Gold Depository;" and "permitted civilian aircraft to land at Fort Knox airfield; use of off-duty military personnel as extras." Since the gold in the depository is the responsibility of the Department of the Treasury, apparently there was no embarrassment to the military.

The Pentagon is quite frank about the role it plays in influencing filmmakers. A statement that accompanied the list of "turn downs" supplied to me said:

When a motion picture project is not favorably considered, this does not imply that the door has been closed irrevocably except in the most unusual circumstances. The producer can make story changes which possibly would qualify the screenplay for consideration of assistance. However, producers usually lose interest or perhaps decide to proceed without Department of Defense assistance. . . . For your information, there are few projects submitted to DoD which can be considered wholly acceptable in accordance with DoD criteria without some revisions. Such changes may be technical or may require plot and/or character revisions. Story conferences ensue and the screenplay is developed to the apparent mutual advantage of the producer or writer and DoD. These projects cannot be considered as "turn downs" and therefore are not listed.

When the Department of Defense is presented with a film project that puts the military in the best light possible, it can go to extraordinary lengths to render assistance. An illustrative example is *The Green Berets,* referred to earlier. The film presents a highly polished image of the Army's Special Forces and their role in the early days of our commitment of troops to combat in Vietnam. The political line of the film is strongly pro-war, and several of the characters deliver long speeches justifying our involvement in it. Illustrative of the content is a scene in which a sergeant dumps an arm-load of captured weapons in front of a dovish newspaper correspondent and shouts, "What's involved here is Communist domination of the world."

Before going to Defense with his project, the star and maker of the film, John Wayne, sent a telegram to President Johnson describing the project and saying he needed Department of Defense assistance. According to the *New York Times,* Bill Moyers replied for the President with a letter in which he said "the President was interested in the project and it sounded like an interesting and exciting venture." The *Times* said that Moyers let the Department of Defense know about the telegram and the letter.

Batjac Productions, Inc., Wayne's filmmaking company, apparently complied with all of the procedures necessary to obtain military clearance which was approved in August 1967. It earlier had provided a staggering list of the physical requirements it needed of the Army. The list was eight pages long and included jeeps, captured Viet Cong weap-

117

ons, American rifles, machine guns, carbines, parachutes, mortars, trucks, tanks, armored personnel carriers, bulldozers, ambulances, helicopters, cargo aircraft, and scout dogs. Without apparent demurrer, the Army made the equipment available at Fort Benning, Georgia, the major shooting location, and at Fort Bragg, North Carolina, and at some nearby airfields where other filming was done.

Wayne's shooting schedule called for forty days of activity on the Army posts. According to a General Accounting Office examination of the Army's involvement with the filmmaking, Batjac was at Fort Benning or at other military installations in the area from August 9, 1967, to November 15, 1967—ninety-eight calendar days. The "requirements" sheets submitted by Wayne's organization indicated that up to 359 Army personnel would be needed to appear on camera, of whom 143 were classified as "permanent." Among those needed were troops of Asian extraction to play roles as Vietnamese—North, South, and Viet Cong. The Army obligingly found a platoon of such troops, men from Hawaii, training at Fort Devens, Massachusetts, and put them on leave status so that Wayne could bring them to Fort Benning to be in the picture. All troops appearing as "extras," from Benning, Bragg, and Devens, were on leave or "off-duty" status. As the Defense Department explains the procedure, "Military personnel whenever they are filmed doing anything above and beyond their normal activities involved in operations or scheduled training are on leave status. Personnel are never ordered to take leave; they do so as they desire and are hired by the producer on a voluntary basis. . ."

Anyone at all familiar with the life of an enlisted service-

118

man knows that leave is sometimes hard to obtain, but apparently there were no obstacles put in the way of the men found suitable by Wayne's company to appear in *The Green Berets*. As for volunteering, since the soldier-extras were paid $1.40 an hour (the minimum Minimum Wage) and their Army pay did not stop, it is doubtful that there were any problems of filling the movie ranks.

Unpaid by Wayne, but paid for by the taxpayers, were the hundreds of troops involved in support functions. According to the General Accounting Office, "Batjac was not charged for military pay costs of troop support furnished by the 10th Aviation Group and the 197th Infantry Brigade of the Infantry Center and of project officers provided by DoD [Department of Defense] and the base commander."* The GAO estimated that this support amounted to 3,800 man-days.

Another requirement that filmmakers supposedly must meet to qualify for military assistance is that there be no interference with normal activities or training if it can be at all avoided. It is hard to believe, however, that the presence of John Wayne's camera crews, electricians, technicians, director, and supernumeraries at Fort Benning, requiring 3,800 man-days of support, plus the use of rifles, mortars, aircraft, bulldozers, cranes, trucks and other arms and equipment did not interfere with the normal tenor of military activities.

Department of Defense Instruction 5410.15 includes among the principles for assistance to nongovernmental film-

---

* According to the GAO, the Fort Benning commander provided an officer and five enlisted men to assist in the production. They spent 107 days at the task.

makers the following: "Diversion of equipment, personnel, and material resources from normal military locations and military operations may be authorized only when circumstances preclude the filming without it, and such diversions shall be held to a minimum and without interference with military operations, and will be on the basis that the production company will reimburse the Government for expenses incurred in the diversion."

The General Accounting Office inquiry found that Wayne was not charged "the loan of weapons, for the use of equipment . . . [or] for 87 flying hours by UH-1 helicopters."

Batjac Productions, Inc., after all was finished paid the U. S. Government $18,623.64. To operate a UH-1 helicopter (the "Huey," extensively used in Vietnam) for 87 hours costs $36,105.

There is a Bureau of the Budget document, Circular A–25, of September 23, 1959, that covers payment to the U.S. Government for assistance such as that given Wayne's commercial enterprise. It says, "Where a service (or privilege) provides special benefits to an identifiable recipient above and beyond that which accrues to the public at large a charge should be imposed to recover the *full cost* to the Federal Government for rendering that service." [Italics mine.]

But the Department of Defense operates by its own rules; Department of Defense Instruction 730.7 of December 20, 1966, set up its own exclusion from the reimbursement requirement for "any service furnished representatives of public information media or the general public *in the interest of public understanding of the Armed Forces.*"

The General Accounting Office coolly observed that the

Department of Defense should make its practices "consistent" with those of the Bureau of the Budget.

While the film was still in production I received from a West Virginia publisher a letter and an editorial he had written questioning the extent of the Army's assistance to Wayne and his company. I passed the question along to Secretary McNamara, and soon had a reply from Phil G. Goulding, then Assistant Secretary for Public Affairs, within whose purview assistance to filmmakers came.

Goulding's letter defended his department's activities and the use of Army equipment saying, "When special or close-up scenes required authentic military material such photography was accommodated only when all material was free of military commitment, and when no private or commercial enterprise could provide same. When expenses to the Government were incurred, the Company reimbursed the Government in full. . . . Assistance to the Batjac Company at Fort Benning was far from unilateral. Upon completion of photography, many truckloads of equipment, training aids, and material as well as a complete Montagnard village constructed at Company expense were presented to the Infantry Center for use in its guerilla warfare training program. Cumulatively, the donation can be evaluated at about $75,000, as estimated by Fort Benning officers, and will result in a significant contribution to the realism and effectiveness of guerilla training conducted at the Center."

At that time, American troops had been in combat in Vietnam for more than two and a half years. If Fort Benning by then did not already have guerilla training facilities as good or better than those left behind by Wayne's company there is something wrong with Army training. Could

121

it be that there was not enough money in the multi-billion-dollar defense budgets of the past several years to have provided the training cadres and the troops under their command those training aids and materials left behind (thereby saving trucking expenses)?

An interesting sidelight on the making of *The Green Berets* appeared in the *New Yorker* after the film opened in New York in the early summer of 1968. Talking to a reporter for the magazine at a party following the premiere, Robin Moore, author of the book from which the film was made, said Wayne's production "caught the spirit of the book but it didn't follow the book. I mean in the book we showed some bad Vietnamese allies. But the movie showed only good ones. The movie should have shown the frustration with the bad Vietnamese. But that was a concession we had to make to the Defense Department. We couldn't have made the film without their approval."

Another recent film to which the Department of Defense lent extraordinary assistance was *Tora! Tora! Tora!*, Darryl F. Zanuck's $20 million depiction of the events leading up to the Japanese attack on Pearl Harbor and of the attack itself. ("Tora" means tiger and was the code word used by the Japanese pilots to signal that the attack had begun.) For the making of this film, Zanuck was given the use of the aircraft carrier U.S.S. *Yorktown,* five other Navy ships in active commission, and two destroyers from the inactive pool—in all, a "task force" of respectable size—and access to facilities in the continental United States and in the Honolulu area.

In the late autumn of 1968, the *Yorktown* sailed out of San Diego bound for Honolulu. She was scheduled to proceed farther into the Pacific to participate in the recovery of Apollo 8 after its lunar-orbit mission. Because of the nature of its duties, the ship did not have the normal complement of aircraft aboard. Instead, she carried forty World War II Japanese planes leased by Zanuck from commercial sources, twenty-nine Navy fliers on "authorized leave or off-duty status" and a number of civilian pilots who were to fly them, and a large deck crew of Marines from El Toro Naval Air Station in California, all experienced in handling aircraft on a carrier and all also "off duty."

Once at sea, with Marines working on deck in Japanese uniforms and the Japanese ensign flying from an appropriately rigged staff, Zanuck's cameras filmed the take-offs of the "enemy strike force" from the *Yorktown's* deck. All the while, according to information given to me by the Department of Defense, the ship "conducted regular scheduled independent ship exercises." Concerning the use of the Japanese ensign that had been reported in the press, Defense took a testy stand.

"It has been implied," it said, "that the U.S.S. *Yorktown* operated under the Japanese national ensign. This is not true. At no time did the U.S.S. *Yorktown* operate under any colors but the U.S. national ensign [American flag]. During WWII, the Japanese national ensign was flown on a shorter staff aft of the island on the flight deck of Japanese carriers. It was from such a mast, constructed by TCF, that the Japanese flag was flown during filming aboard the U.S.S. *Yorktown* while the American ensign flew from its appropriate mast."

Once the film company got to Honolulu additional large demands were made on naval personnel and facilities. The

123

"Japanese" planes used Barber's Point Naval Air Station as a base and from this field the simulated attacks on Pearl Harbor were flown. An ammunition lighter "not scheduled for Navy use during the production period" was loaned to the company to support a mock-up of the battleship U.S.S. *Arizona*, sunk in the attack; a Navy helicopter squadron took "training advantage of lifting externals loads" and moved eighteen full-scale models of P-40 fighters about five miles from dock to Wheeler Air Force Base; the schedules of several ships were altered to permit filming, and various base facilities were put at Zanuck's disposal.

Perhaps prompted by criticisms of the amount of money John Wayne was charged for assistance given to *The Green Berets*, the bill for Zanuck's use of the *Yorktown*, his "task force," and for other facilities was a sizeable one —$319,091 for "equipment, fuel consumption, maintenance and services, military labor and materiel, safety observers, parking fees, and related activities," and for transporting the Japanese planes from San Diego to Honolulu. The General Accounting Office says that the Navy's bill should have been $196,000 higher, and admirals appearing before the House Subcommittee on Defense Appropriations in February 1970 were asked what they were going to do about it. As far as I know the Navy had not come up with an answer.

Sizeable as the total of these amounts is, one wonders if they fully covered the costs of interference with normal naval operations and what a commercial organization would call "overhead charges." But apparently this aspect of military participation in *Tora! Tora! Tora!* did not bother the Navy. When the proposal first arose that Zanuck be loaned an aircraft carrier, Deputy Secretary of Defense Paul H. Nitze, a former Secretary of the Navy; his successor, Paul R. Ignatius, and top admirals supported the idea, according to participants in the discussions. On a television broadcast in May of 1969 Arthur Sylvester, who had been Assistant Secretary of Defense for Public Affairs at the time Zanuck's film proposal was first presented for assistance, said the Navy thought the publicity for military preparedness was worth the risk of criticism.

Nearly twenty-nine years have passed since Pearl Harbor. American feelings toward the Japanese are no longer inimical. But the propriety of promoting preparedness by reconstructing the attack of December 7, 1941, even in the climate of present-day good feelings, is open to question. Perhaps in Zanuck's case, the instruction was considered retroactively, for he also produced *The Longest Day,* a star-emblazoned story of the Allied invasion of France in World War II. Interestingly, however, assistance given to him for that film raised questions also, since some 700 combat troops were brought from Germany to act in it—at a time when President Kennedy was calling up National Guardsmen and Reservists for duty because of the Berlin Crisis.

8 | Sound Off

HISTORICALLY, THERE HAVE BEEN BARRIERS in the United States against the military establishment's acquiring political influence. These barriers have been anchored in the country's non-military traditions, the principle of civilian supremacy, and the fact that until World War II we never tried to maintain a large permanent military force.

Today, however, as a result of thirty years of hot and cold war, the military has become an active participant in national policy processes. The influence of the Defense Department and its component parts in making national policy is not limited to Presidents, Secretaries of State, and the military and foreign policy committees of the Congress. This influence extends also to the "think tanks" and universities to which Defense parcels out lucrative research grants, to the corporations and labor unions which profit from Defense contracts, and as preceding pages of this book have tried to demonstrate, to public opinion.

Besides using all of the modern tools for opinion molding, the military makes use also of the oldest—public speaking. In earlier chapters I recited the numbers of speakers who tour the country selling the military line—one thousand a month within one Army command alone. Such saturation is easily possible, for there is an almost limitless supply of high-level talent. There are 29 four-star generals, 94 lieutenant generals, 7 admirals, 41 vice admirals, and 1,339 other officers of flag rank (brigadier and major generals and rear admirals) in the Army, Air Force, Marine Corps, and Navy, who when not plying their basic trades are available for speaking engagements.

At any and all times, whatever the audience or occasion, it can be assumed that a military speaker is supporting the policies and programs of the Department of Defense and his own service—with the exception of a very few unusual men like General Shoup who is now retired. There is no significant variation from a basic line; there may be some who don't agree, but they don't make speeches.

As noted earlier, there are restrictions imposed on military speakers by service regulations. In brief, they are supposed to keep their remarks within the limits of their own competence and experience and within the limits of stated national policy. Also, there are special restrictions concerning speeches or remarks about the Vietnam war, with discussion of its foreign policy implications prohibited. However, all of the regulations seem to become elastic when high-ranking officers are involved, and even within the strict limits of regulations some of the statements of these officers are often of dubious propriety.

A story in the *Evening Star,* Washington, D.C., in November 1969, quoted a number of such statements. In part the story said:

While President Nixon has been seeking support for his efforts to win the Vietnam war, high ranking Pentagon officers have been out giving the word to the "silent majority."

In an almost steady stream, they have been speaking to Rotary Clubs, Reserve Officers meetings, at ship launchings, and almost anywhere a responsive audience might be expected to gather.

Frequently they have taken a tough line—using language more forceful than the President and even outdoing Vice President Spiro T. Agnew on occasion, according to a spot check of speeches delivered over the last two months.

Speaking to the Association of the U.S. Army here on October 15, for example, General Earle C. Wheeler, chairman of the Joint Chiefs of Staff, referred caustically to "groups of interminably vocal youngsters, strangers alike to soap and reason . . ."

"For my part, I must confess to be a bit fatigued on this score when new words are produced, most often by the 'academic-journalistic' complex, which describe vacillation as being flexible and nervousness as being compassionate."

The story goes on to quote remarks similar in tone if not in substance made in other speeches by General Leonard F. Chapman, Jr., commandant of the Marine Corps; by his deputy, General Lewis W. Walt; and by Admiral John S. McCain, Jr., commander of all U.S. forces in the Pacific.

The "tough line" discerned by the *Star* reporter also runs through almost all of a dozen speeches by high-ranking officers that were supplied to me by the Pentagon. In several, the news media are accused of overplaying dissent against our Vietnam policy and not paying enough attention to the "good" in our society. In others, "self-styled experts" are chided. Those who protest quietly against the

129

war are recognized as "people of peace," but are labeled as supporters of "peace at any price." There is criticism of "anti-everything organizations" who oppose our involvement "only because they are in accord with the principles of the enemy." And the bogeyman of the "world-wide Communist conspiracy" is brought out to buttress the argument, as the *Star* story also noted:

In general, the professional military men tend to see the threat of communism as somewhat more menacing than many political leaders.

Speaking at the launching of a destroyer named for his father, Admiral John S. McCain, Jr., commander of the Pacific command, said September 6 at the Philadelphia Navy Yard:

"What we do here today is related to a subject that should be of direct concern to every American. That topic is the threat of aggressive communism as it affects the peace of the world and American national security.

"We must be aware of the continuing threat which our country faces from the ambitions, goals, and activities of the Communist world. This is a real threat and a stark truth that we must recognize if there is to be peace."

The speeches I have examined are uniformly didactic about the war in Vietnam and the President's Vietnamization program and are almost unctuously self-righteous about the role we are playing there. General Westmoreland told an Army-Industry dinner in Dallas in November 1969, "Contrary to some reports, our shield of military power has not laid waste to Vietnam." He then went on to talk about medical aid being given to "thousands who had never seen a doctor" and of the hundreds of schools, market places, and meeting houses being built by our troops. Nowhere in the Dallas speech, or in speeches in Pittsburgh, Philadelphia,

Savannah, Georgia, and Greenwood, South Carolina—all made in the course of one month—did General Westmoreland mention that more than 40,000 American troops have died in combat or that hundreds of thousands of Vietnamese civilians, both North and South, have also been casualties.

In the Greenwood speech before a home-state audience, General Westmoreland again emphasized our nation-building role in Vietnam, then went after the critics.

I am personally concerned by the continual protest against those who accept the responsibilities of leadership and who are doing their utmost to bring about an honorable peace. . . . Outbursts and derision should not be against our national policies arrived at through constitutional means. In my opinion, if the demonstration of last Wednesday* had been in support of our President, peace would be nearer at hand. . . .

Today it would seem that the words "patriotism," "the Defense Establishment," "law and order," "draft," "obedience," "responsibility," have become odious. . . .

Just recently I returned from Europe where I visited the United Kingdom. I spoke with some community leaders there who were perplexed and confounded by the havoc and bloodshed in Ireland. They questioned, "Where did we go wrong? What have we done that citizens of the same country and of the same race, differing only in religion, should fight and destroy property and one another?" Had it not been for the forces of law and order—the British military and local police—Belfast may well have burned to the ground. . . .

Could this happen in the United States of America? I believe that it can. We have seen something like it in the smoke and fire of the long hot summer of 1968. Yes, the enemy got into the outskirts of Saigon but in Washington our own citizens tried to destroy our capital city.

* The October 15, 1969, Moratorium March in Washington.

This kind of oversimplification is not an isolated example. The night before Westmoreland's speech in South Carolina, General James K. Woolnough, head of the United States Continental Army Command—our home-based Army troops—spoke to the Baltimore USO Council. After referring to violence around the world and on American campuses and in our cities, he said:

Amid this scene of violence and threats to our national security around the world, what is the focus of the attacks of militant radicals, supported by much of the news media—who are the "bad guys" who are the targets of these attacks?

Isn't it really a little amazing that it is the one single force in our nation that can insure national security, internal as well as external—the so-called military-industrial complex which in the perilous days of World War II was referred to as the "Arsenal of Democracy" by President Roosevelt.

I wonder how many Americans realize the fact that only last year the uniformed forces alone stood between some of our greatest cities, including our National Capital, and anarchy in the rioting that followed the assassination of Dr. Martin Luther King?

One wonders how many other military men may be expounding similar views about the Army's "internal" role. The Marines' General Walt, who has been delivering the same basic speech for more than three years on an average of twice a week, concentrates on dissent, its effect on the Vietnam war, and the threat of "international communism."

"Without dissent, I believe the war would have been over a year ago," he told the state convention of the Florida Red Cross at Daytona Beach, October 10, 1969. "It would be history instead of the current bloody conflict.

"In the past year over 10,000 Americans have been killed in Vietnam. Those who dissent may not have fired a rifle or thrown a grenade, but they must bear a part of the responsibility for the loss of those gallant Americans."

In Pensacola, Florida, on October 21 he said, "We hear a great deal about dissent these days. For some people in this country, it has become an end in itself. There was a time in this country when a person who opposed our institutions and duly constituted authority was called an anarchist—now he is a dissenter."

At the Rotary Club of Annapolis, Maryland, two weeks later the general made similar remarks about dissent and dissenters with additional emphasis on "international communism."

"Our loss of Vietnam" [he said], "would only confirm the Communist claim that they can eventually take over the entire world by their technique of sponsoring wars of national liberation. . . . We must come to the aid of those countries whose security and freedom are important to the security of the United States. If we are not to be engulfed we must make a stand somewhere. Where shall we stand if not in Vietnam? . . . If we don't stop Communist aggression wherever and whenever it takes place today, our next generation will be fighting a lot tougher enemy a lot closer to home."

The Navy's Office of Information every two years publishes a booklet titled "Outstanding Navy Speeches." In the issue currently in use, the Navy Chief of Information says in a preface, "Navy men and women are delivering more and better public speeches than ever before. The seventeen manuscripts included in this collection are believed to offer many ideas which can be incorporated in future speeches." A version of the Walt speech, which he delivered to the Alumni Association of the Industrial Col-

133

lege of the Armed Forces, is one of those rating the accolade of "Outstanding."

Not only high-ranking officers of the armed services travel the country at taxpayers' expense to propound the military line on Vietnam, but enlisted men are used as well. The Army has a special speakers program that sends Vietnam veterans on regional tours "to further the Army image" and "to bring the story of the Army in Vietnam to the grassroots level," as one of the speakers put it. According to newspaper reports from my home state of Arkansas, one of these speakers is Specialist First Class Carrol V. Dewees, who is stationed at Fort Sill, Oklahoma, and who travels Oklahoma, Arkansas, and Texas. Although U.S. policy, set by the President, is "to end the war in Vietnam, preferably by negotiations, as soon as possible," Sergeant Dewees, using a speech without doubt prepared by the Army, was quoted as saying that he "can't see where anything is going to be accomplished in Paris." Further, he is reported to have said, "To leave Vietnam to its fate now would shake the confidence of all those people [who "count on us" against Communist aggression] in the value of an American commitment and the value of the American word."

The entrance of the military establishment into the field of foreign affairs over the past twenty years has resulted in a requirement by the Department of State that speeches and articles by the military involving questions of foreign policy be cleared "to ensure that when the information in this material is given to the public it is accurate as to facts, it correctly expresses United States policy, and it does not include statements which might be damaging to the foreign relations of the United States." These criteria would seem to be explicit enough to keep the military in line. The review process, too, is a thorough one, extending as necessary through the department's bureau of public affairs, to the public affairs advisers of the geographic and functional bureaus, to specific area experts as necessary. That review itself is necessary seems to be demonstrated by State's reactions to 124 manuscripts submitted to it by flag officers during a recent eight-month period. Two of the speeches were found to be objectionable "in their entirety," in sixteen cases "mandatory" changes were needed, in forty-eight cases "discretionary" changes were made, and in twenty-eight cases, for reasons of accuracy or clarity, changes were proposed. Only thirty of the manuscripts, fewer than one-quarter of the total, needed no changes at all.

In response to a query about the effectiveness of the clearance process on the product given to the public, Deputy Undersecretary William B. Macomber, who at the time was Assistant Secretary for Congressional Relations, said that State has no records of whether proposed changes were made or not.

"However," he wrote, "no case has come to our attention where a mandatory change was ignored, and it is our impression that our recommended changes are generally accepted."

State's "impression" of the military's acceptance of its recommended changes may be generally correct, but on occasion recommendations are largely ignored. A case in point is an interview with Admiral McCain published in the February 1969 *Reader's Digest*. The text of the inter-

135

view, cabled from the admiral's headquarters in Hawaii, was reviewed by State and cleared for publication subject to a dozen "recommended" changes. When the issue of the magazine reached the newsstands, it was found that only four of the changes had been made.

Reader's Digest has the largest circulation of any publication in the United States and its foreign editions have readers numbered in the millions. All of these readers had set before them Admiral McCain's opinion of the military situation in Vietnam. The Admiral said:

"We have the enemy licked now. He is beaten. We have the initiative in all areas. The enemy cannot achieve a military victory; he cannot even mount another major offensive. We are in the process of eliminating his remaining capability to threaten the security of South Vietnam. I am convinced that that is why he has come to the conference table in Paris—to try to win there what he failed to win on the battlefields . . ."

The State Department's demurrer to this statement did not touch on the damage that these words might have on delicate negotiations then in progress. It was based on the domestic reaction to the first sentence, "We have the enemy licked now."

"The existing language," the State Department review memorandum said, "might be questioned by Americans who will ask how a beaten enemy can mount a new offensive even if it is a minor one, or continue the hard fighting mentioned later . . ."

This is a sensible enough observation, but it does not touch on the foreign policy question involved. The other

136

changes proposed for the article were similarly cautious "recommendations" rather than mandatory changes.

The erosion of the State Department's pre-eminence as the foreign policy arm of the government ought to be stopped. To stop it State must establish its position once and for all and it should not be the kind expressed in a letter I received from Mr. Macomber when I questioned the propriety of Admiral McCain's remarks. Mr. Macomber wrote:

"The Department expects that the assessments of a military situation by a military officer, as expressed in a speech or article, may often differ from that of the Department. When there is no significant difference between the statements of a military officer and established United States policy, and when in our opinion these statements do not appear likely to damage the country's foreign relations, we are reluctant to propose mandatory amendments in our review. We often recommend changes, offering strong reasons for them, as we did in the interview of Admiral McCain."

Something more than the expression of "strong reasons" is apparently needed to re-establish the proper bounds between our government's foreign policy arm and the military establishment.

The State Department review process did succeed in softening one of Admiral McCain's answers, an answer that reflected a point of view similar to that he expressed at the destroyer launching in Philadelphia.

"Do you have any advice for a war-weary American people?" he was asked by the *Digest* interviewer.

The beginning of the reply to this question as received

137

from Honolulu was: "Yes. A major portion of this war has actually been fought in the United States. In fact, the Communists hoped to win it there, and now that their military situation is hopeless they are determined to win it there. The American people have been subjected to the best conceived and most highly efficient propaganda campaign over this war that they have ever been up against. This campaign has created deep divisions in our country, divisions which inevitably have severely hampered the efforts to achieve an acceptable peaceful settlement . . ."

The State Department's reaction was "The existing language . . . credits Communist propaganda with exerting a greater influence than it really has upon the thinking of the critics of U.S. policy with respect of Vietnam." The Admiral dropped the quoted portion of the answer, and kept in the interview his views on the dangers of "wars of national liberation."

The view Admiral McCain expressed is shared by many military men who hold that critics of the government's Vietnam policy, whatever their credentials, play into the hands of the enemy and prolong the war. Military speeches on the subject are larded with invidious references to long-haired young men, the press, the academic community, "so-called experts," and, usually in veiled form, members of the Congress.

Some of the remarks made by the military about the Congress are not even veiled. Major James N. Rowe, a Special Forces officer who spent more than five years as a prisoner of the Viet Cong before he escaped in December 1968, has impugned the motives of some members of the Senate and criticized the news media's handling of news

138

about Vietnam. Ten months after his escape, Major Rowe began appearing on television programs made by members of the House of Representatives for home consumption. According to the *Washington Post*, he participated in at least twenty television interviews and six radio programs with these Congressmen.

"On several shows," the *Post* story said, "he has questioned the patriotism of Sen. George McGovern. Rowe also has said that his captors exploited the statements of Sens. J. W. Fulbright, Mike Mansfield, and former Sen. Wayne Morse.

"He regularly charges the *Washington Post*, the *New York Times*, the Associated Press, United Press International, *Look, Time,* and *Life* with supplying materials that break the morale of American prisoners."

Major Rowe's sudden appearance on the Washington scene, according to the Pentagon, arose from his being invited to lecture at the State Department's Foreign Service Institute about his experiences in Vietnam. During his visit, which was prolonged with Army approval, he appeared before a special session of the House Armed Services Committee, had a meeting with General Westmoreland, and spent twenty-five minutes with President Nixon, besides making the television and radio tapes for Congressmen's "home town reports."

The *Post* reporter who monitored the tapes he made wrote that the major mentioned that Vietcong flags were flown at the Washington Monument grounds during the November 15 peace demonstration. "One thing that stood out," he said, was Senator McGovern's remark at the rally that the protestors "cherish the flag."

"I wonder what flag did he cherish. What flag did they [the protestors] cherish?"

When I queried the Department of Defense about Major Rowe's reported statements, I received a reply from Brigadier General Leon E. Benade, a deputy assistant secretary, generally defending them.

The Army made a check of all interviews in which Major Rowe has participated and I think it is fair to say that these interviews reflect his experience while a prisoner of war, with major topics being his capture, treatment, indoctrination, and escape. It is true that in several of these interviews he stated that the communists stopped using their own sources of propaganda in late 1967 and began to quote leading United States Government figures and news media instead. In this context Major Rowe did mention the names of certain public officials and news media. In one interview Major Rowe made a personal comment, not based on his experience as a prisoner, about a Senator's remarks that protestors "cherish the flag." It has been called to Major Rowe's attention that, while he has a right to express personal opinions, he should avoid doing so in a manner or a context that might cause his personal opinion to be interpreted as official policy or comment.

9 | Dangers of the Military Sell

ALTHOUGH I CANNOT CONCEIVE of a single top-ranking officer in any of the armed services who today would consider an attempt to overturn our constitutional government—in the manner of *Seven Days in May* fiction—militarism as a philosophy poses a distinct threat to our democracy. At the minimum, it represents a dangerously constricted but highly influential point of view when focussed on our foreign relations. It is a viewpoint that by its nature takes little account of political and moral complexities, even less of social and economic factors, and almost no account of human and psychological considerations.

Rarely does a general officer invoke the higher loyalty of patriotism—his own concept of it, that is—over loyalty to civilian political authority, as General MacArthur did in his defiance of President Truman.* But if, as time goes on, our country continues to be chronically at war, continues to neglect its domestic problems, and continues to have unrest in cities and on campuses, then militarism will surely increase. And even if the military itself does not take over the government directly, it could—because of increasing use in domestic crises—come to acquire power comparable to that of the German General Staff in the years before World War I. I hope this never comes to pass. It may not seem likely now, but it is by no means so inconceivable that we need not warn against it and act to prevent it.

I have often warned those students who talk of the need to revise our system by revolution that if such a revolution were to take place, the government that would emerge for our country would not be the one they seek. It would rather be authoritarian and controlled by the very forces who today promote military solutions to foreign policy problems.

The leadership of professional military officer corps stems from a few thousand high-ranking officers of unusual ability and energy that comes of single-mindedness. Marked as men of talents by their rise to the highest ranks through the rigorous competitiveness of the military services, they bring to bear a strength in conviction and a near unanimity of outlook that gives them an influence, in government councils and in Congress, on public policy disproportionate to their numbers. Disciplined and loyal to their respective services, with added prestige derived from heroic combat

* *The MacArthur Story,* a film version of the glamorous general's life made by the Office of Information for the Armed Forces, is available to the public in military film libraries.

records, they operate with an efficiency not often found among civilian officials.

The danger to public policy arises from civilian authorities adopting the narrowness of outlook of professional soldiers—an outlook restricted by training and experience to the use of force. As we have developed into a society whose most prominent business is violence, one of the leading professions inevitably is soldiering. Since they are the professionals, and civilian bureaucrats refuse to challenge them, the military have become ardent and effective competitors for power in American society.

The services compete with each other for funds, for the control of weapons systems, and for the privilege of being "first to fight." Constantly improving their techniques for rapid deployment, they not only yearn to try them out but when opportunities arise they press their proposals on civilian authorities. The latter group all too often is tempted by the seemingly quick "surgical" course of action proposed by the military in preference to the long and wearisome methods of diplomacy. For a variety of reasons— from believing it the only course of action to testing equipment and techniques of counterinsurgency, or just to avoid the disgrace of being "left out"—all the military services were enthusiastic about the initial involvement in Vietnam. By now they should have had their fill, but they still push on, trying out new weapons and new strategies—such as "destroying sanctuaries" in Cambodia.

The root cause of militarism is war, and so long as we have the one we will be menaced by the other. The best defense against militarism is peace; the next best thing is the vigorous practice of democracy. The dissent against our government's actions in Southeast Asia, the opposition to the ABM and MIRV, and the increased willingness of many in the Congress to do something about the hitherto sacrosanct military budget are all encouraging signs of democracy being practiced. But there is much in American polity these days that is discouraging.

There seems to be a lack of concern among too many people about the state of the nation, and a too easy acceptance of policies and actions of a kind that a generation ago would have appalled the citizenry. The apparent broad acceptance of the "volunteer army" idea comes to mind— a concept completely at variance with our historic development. Up to now, a blessing of our system has been that those who go into the military service, whether by enlistment or through the draft, could hardly wait to get out.* But today, because of the exigencies of the times, there is a chance that we may turn our back on this fundamental principle: a large, standing professional army has no place in this Republic.

Along with promoting militarism as part of our society, the mindless violence of war has eaten away at our moral values as well as our sensitivity. Reporters covering the domestic aspects of the My Lai massacre story in the home area of Lieutenant Robert Calley were surprised to find loud support for the accused—not sympathy, which might be expected, but support. Among these people there seemed to be no recognition of possible wrongdoing or criminal act in the alleged massacre.

---

* Despite attractive re-enlistment bonuses, the Army's rate of retention in 1969 of men finishing their first term is 14.6 percent for volunteers and 7.4 percent for draftees.

Beyond the discouragements—and even the disturbing things such as the Cambodian adventure and our activities in Thailand and Laos—one has to hope, with reason drawn from our history, that the traditional workings of our system and the innate common sense of Americans will prevail. The task certainly is not going to be easy. We have been so stunned, almost desensitized—like Lieutenant Calley's supporters—by what has gone on during the recent past that it is almost possible to turn to total pessimism. History did not prepare the American people for the imperial role in which we find ourselves, and we are paying a moral price for it. From the time of the framing of our Constitution to the two world wars, our experience and values—if not our uniform practice—conditioned us not for the unilateral exercise of power but for the placing of limits upon it. Perhaps it was vanity, but we supposed that we could be an example for the world—an example of rationality and restraint.

Our practice has not lived up to that ideal but, from the earliest days of the Republic, the ideal has retained its hold upon us, and every time we have acted inconsistently with it—not just in Vietnam and Cambodia—a hue and cry of opposition has arisen. When the United States invaded Mexico two former Presidents and a future one—John Quincy Adams, Van Buren, and Lincoln—denounced the war as violating American principles. Adams, the senior of them, is even said to have expressed the hope that General Taylor's officers would resign and his men desert. When the United States fought a war with Spain and then suppressed the patriotic resistance of the Philippines, the ranks of opposition numbered two former Presidents—

145

Harrison and Cleveland—Senators and Congressmen, including the Speaker of the House of Representatives, and such distinguished—and differing—individuals as Andrew Carnegie and Samuel Gompers.

The incongruity between our old values and the new unilateral power we wield has greatly troubled the American people. It has much to do, I suspect, with the current student rebellion. Like a human body reacting against a transplanted organ, our body politic is reacting against the alien values which, in the name of security, have been grafted upon it. We cannot, and dare not, divest ourselves of power, but we have a choice as to how we will use it. We can try to ride out the current convulsion in our society and adapt ourselves to a new role as the world's nuclear vigilante. Or we can try to adapt our power to our traditional values, never allowing it to become more than a means toward domestic societal ends, while seeking every opportunity to discipline it within an international community.

It is not going to help us to reach these ends to have a president fearful that we are going to be "humiliated," nor for him to turn to the military as a prime source of advice on foreign affairs. In the case of Cambodia the President accepted military advice during the decision-making process, apparently in preference to that of the Department of State, thereby turning to an initial military solution rather than a diplomatic or political one. Of course the Senate was not consulted. Once the treaty power of the Senate was regarded as the only constitutional means of making a significant foreign commitment, while executive agreements in foreign affairs were confined to matters of routine. Today the treaty has been reduced to only one of a number of methods of entering binding foreign engagements. In current usage the term "commitment" is used less often to refer to obligations deriving from treaties than to those deriving from executive agreements and even simple, sometimes casual declarations.

Thailand provides an interesting illustration. Under the SEATO Treaty, the United States has only two specific obligations to Thailand: to act "in accordance with its constitutional processes" in the event that Thailand is overtly attacked, and to "consult immediately" with the other SEATO allies should Thailand be threatened by subversion. But the presence of 40,000 American troops, assigned there by the executive acting entirely on its own authority, creates a *de facto* commitment going far beyond the SEATO Treaty, a commitment largely based on military recommendations and desires. On March 6, 1962, Secretary of State Dean Rusk and Thai Foreign Minister Thanat Khoman issued a joint declaration in which Secretary Rusk expressed "the firm intention of the United States to aid Thailand, its ally and historic friend, in resisting Communist aggression and subversion." Obviously this goes far beyond the SEATO Treaty and omits any reference to Constitutional processes.

An even more striking illustration of the upgrading of a limited agreement into a *de facto* defense obligation is provided by the series of agreements negotiated over the past sixteen years for the maintenance of bases in Spain. Initiated under an executive agreement in 1953, the bases agreement was significantly upgraded by a joint declaration issued by Secretary Rusk and Spanish Foreign Minister

147

Castiella in 1963 asserting that a "threat to either country" would be an occasion for each to "take such action as it may consider necessary within its constitutional processes." In strict constitutional law, this agreement, whose phrasing closely resembles that of our multilateral security treaties, would be binding on no one excepting Private Citizen Rusk; in fact it is what might be called the "functional equivalent" of a treaty ratified by the Senate. Acknowledging even more explicitly the extent of our *de facto* commitment to Spain, General Earle Wheeler, then Chairman of the Joint Chiefs of Staff, acting under instructions from Secretary Rusk, provided Spanish military authorities in 1968 with a secret memorandum asserting that the presence of American armed forces in Spain—like the ones who participated in *Exercise Pathfinder Express* described in chapter six—constituted a more significant security guarantee than would a written agreement. Again, as with the Thai commitment, strategic military considerations, arrived at by military commanders with the acquiesence of civilian authorities undoubtedly were the overriding factors in the political decision.

The Department of State is not alone among the agencies of government awed as well as outmanned, outmaneuvered, or simply elbowed aside by executive military decision-making. The Defense Department has established a massive bureaucracy, like that at the Department of Commerce, the Atomic Energy Commission, the Department of Health, Education, and Welfare, and all the rest who protect their positions and interests within the mechanism of governmental power and appropriations.

When war was abhorrent to the American people, the

military was considered only as a tool to be used if needed. Today, with our chronic state of war, and with peace becoming the unusual, the military has created for itself an image as a comforting thing to have around. In reality, however, it has become a monster bureaucracy that can grind beneath its wheels the other bureaucracies, whatever their prescribed roles in the process of government and their legitimate needs.

One of the arms of the Defense Department monster bureaucracy is the military public relations apparatus that today is selling the Administration's Southeast Asia policy, just as it sold the Vietnam policy of the previous Administration, with increasing emphasis on patriotic militarism and activity directed against its critics. The enthusiasm and dedication of the purveyors of the hard military line are such that their present course could easily be changed so as to direct attention to the removal of those in the Congress who question actions of the executive branch and the growth of military influence.

Considering the normal skepticism of the American citizen, such overt political activity by the military would seem to have small chance of success. But I raise the point, nevertheless; the apparatus exists, and we of the Congress, in another context, have been put on notice that legitimate, and even constitutionally required questioning is viewed by some as interference with executive prerogatives.

It is interesting to compare American government's only *official* propaganda organization, the U.S. Information Agency, with the Defense Department's apparatus. USIA is so circumscribed by Congress that it cannot, with the rarest of exceptions, distribute its materials within this

149

country. Since much USIA output is composed of a filtered view of the United States and its policies, such a prohibition is eminently sensible. But the Defense Department, with more than twice as many people engaged in public relations as USIA has in all of its posts abroad, operates to distribute its propaganda within this country without control other than the executive, and floods the domestic scene with its special, narrow view of the military establishment and its role in the world.

Of course the military needs an information program. But it should be one designed to inform, not promote or possibly deceive. There is no need for production of self-promotional films for public consumption. There is no need for flying private citizens about the country to demonstrate to them our military might. There is no need for sending speakers at taxpayers' expense anywhere from Pensacola, Florida, to Portland, Oregon, to talk to luncheon clubs and veterans organizations. There is no need for setting up expensive and elaborate exhibits at state and county fairs. There is no need for taking VIP's on pleasant cruises to Hawaii aboard aircraft carriers. There is no need for "Red," "White," and "Blue" teams criss-crossing the country, "educating" people about the dangers of communism, the need for patriotism, and the Gross National Product of newly independent lands. There certainly is no need for military production of television shows for domestic, commercial use showing "feature" aspects of the Southeast Asian war.

What can be done about the situation?

An obvious answer comes at once to mind—legislation that would again set a ceiling on Defense Department public relations spending. It didn't work before, but perhaps this time it might be possible to require the Defense Department to report on a regular basis to the Congress and to the public on just what it is doing in the "information" field. Such legislation might also eliminate some of the activities that are far outside the military's proper role in our society—such as the "V-Series" films from Southeast Asia and the "educational" programs of the Industrial College of the Armed Forces. It also might require the State Department to enforce strict clearance of films, speeches, and other material involving foreign policy.

The passage of such legislation would be desirable, but only as a step toward limiting the other activities in which the Pentagon is engaged far beyond the true mission assigned—of physically protecting the country.

The real solution to militarism, of course, requires a central attack on the previously uncontrolled size of the military establishment. The growth of the military attitude began in perilous times when an implacable Stalin and world communism were a major threat to the noncommunist world recovering from a devastating war. But the growth of real Pentagon political power did not begin until we became increasingly involved in Vietnam seven years ago. Although the Congress these days is looking more coolly at the enormous defense budget than it has in the past, the surgical process of cutting back will be a difficult one—and not popular with many members to whose districts the military-industrial establishment has become of very great economic importance.

It may help if the public starts examining carefully attempts by the military to sell them its point of view. The

151

press, radio, and television might look more critically on the military's attempts to influence or use them. Not that the media have been remiss in their responsibilities. The exposure of the Starbird Memorandum, for example, was a very real service, and frequently the press has been the only source of real information about what is going on in Southeast Asia and throughout the world. But there are some who allow themselves to be seduced by the military with free trips and VIP treatment, and even a few who are not much more than trained seals for the Pentagon. Also, there are editors who are not skeptical enough about the material fed to them by the military. Radio and television, as we have seen, are heavy users of the military's propaganda and public relations output. Perhaps some of their executives should devote more attention to filling their "public service" time examining the grave domestic problems besetting the country instead of using "V-Films" and the Army's "Big Picture."

Nearly ten years ago I made a speech to the National War College and the Industrial College of the Armed Forces in Washington. I said:

The effectiveness of our armed services depends upon the maintenance of their unique prestige and integrity. These will remain intact only so long as the services adhere to their tradition of nonpolitical professionalism. No group or institution can participate in political debate without itself becoming an object of partisan attack. It is precisely because of its status as a nonpolitical institution that the military in the past has enjoyed the virtually unanimous support of the American people and has thus been beyond partisan assault. . . . It is my hope that the armed services will never yield to misguided temptations which can only shatter the high esteem in which they are held. The preservation of that esteem is essential to the success of the armed forces in fulfilling their assigned mission and essential also, therefore, to the defense of the Republic.

Since I made that speech in 1961, the military has been dragged into the political arena. President Johnson at one crisis point brought General Westmoreland from Saigon to address a joint session of the Congress, in order to counter critics in the Senate with an honored officer's explanation as a means of selling administration policy. What troubles me today is that some politicians want to use the military in such a role, and will be loath to give it up.

An indication—let us say a hint—of some in the military's liking that role is contained in the "Prize Essay 1970" printed in the March 1970 issue of *U.S. Naval Institute Proceedings,* a semi-official learned journal on naval affairs printed in Annapolis, Maryland.

The prize essay, chosen presumably by a high-ranking group of naval officers, is titled "Against All Enemies," and was written by Captain Robert J. Hanks, USN, commander of a destroyer squadron who earlier served in the Pentagon. The theme of his essay is that the military must determine the nature and extent of external threats against our national security, and must also determine the character of our response to them. Captain Hanks also wrote that there are many individuals in the country who want to curb the military, including a fair sampling of the Senate. He names Senators Clifford P. Case and Walter F. Mondale, who have questioned the need for more aircraft carriers, Mike Mansfield and Stuart Symington, who wonder about the size of our troop levels in Europe, Charles E. Goodell, who proposed withdrawal of our troops from Vietnam by December 1, 1970, and myself—people who he wrote, would, in effect, "so weaken this nation's defenses as to place the United States in the greatest jeopardy in its history."

Captain Hanks also came to the conclusion that "while the threat from without remains, we now face an equally potent challenge from within. . . . In concentrating on the main task of the past 30 years—the external threat—some of us may have forgotten that we solemnly swore to support and defend the Constitution of the United States against all enemies, foreign *and domestic*." [Italics are Captain Hanks'.]—And, "If the United States is to be protected against efforts of those who would place her in peril—through apathy, ignorance, or malice—we of the military cannot stand idly, silently by and watch it done. Our oath of office will not permit it."

A real hope in the fight against military influence, I believe, rests with our young. War is abhorrent to them as it seemingly is not to many of us who have lived with slaughter for the past thirty years and made an apparent accommodation to the threat of nuclear destruction. The young remain unpersuaded that man is brought upon this earth solely to find his way to the grave. There is among them a vigorous affirmation of life, a love of life that is optimistic and confident of the future. The anti-life philosophy of militarism offends their minds and hearts.

An observation so widely cited that it is almost an axiom is that no one hates war more than the professional soldier. I think de Tocqueville was closer to the mark when he wrote:

. . . all the ambitious minds in a democratic army ardently long for war, because war makes vacancies [for promotion] available

154

and at last allows violations of the rule of seniority, which is the one privilege natural to a democracy. We thus arrive at the strange conclusion that of all armies those which long for war most ardently are the democratic ones, but that of all peoples those most deeply attached to peace are the democratic nations. And the most extraordinary thing about the whole matter is that it is equality which is responsible for both these contradictory results.*

Beyond the ambition of which de Tocqueville wrote, there is even more danger to our democracy from the dehumanizing kind of war we are fighting that produces among the military an insensitivity to life hard for the civilian to comprehend. We have fought many wars before, but none since our Revolution has lasted as long as the present one. Officers and noncoms go back to Southeast Asia for second and third tours of duty, to engage in second and third rounds of killing. Such long immersion in violence of the kind peculiar to this war cannot but brutalize many of those who go through it. *Harper's* magazine in its May 1970 issue ran an excerpt from Seymour M. Hersh's book on the My Lai massacre.**

Hersh wrote, "One brigade commander ran a contest to celebrate his unit's 10,000th enemy kill. The winning GI received a week's pass to stay in the colonel's personal quarters. Many battalions staged contests among their rifle companies for the highest score in enemy kills, with the winning unit getting additional time for passes." I recall nothing during World War II that equals in callousness a statement that Hersh attributes to the colonel-son of a fa-

* de Tocqueville, *Democracy in America*, pp. 622–623.

** *My Lai 4: A Report on the Massacre and its Aftermath* (New York: Random House, 1970).

155

mous general: "I do like to see the arms and legs fly." Horrifying words, but no more so than the euphemisms "body count," "free-fire zone," and others the military use to camouflage their deadly business.

Perhaps there is something in the theory advanced by psychologist Erich Fromm that in men there are polar attitudes toward life, "biophilia" (love of life) and "necrophilia" (love of death). Spinoza in his *Ethics,* Fromm says, epitomized the spirit of the biophile: "A freeman thinks of death least of all things and his wisdom is a dedication not of death but of life." The necrophile, on the other hand, has values precisely the reverse, for death, not life, excites and satisfies him. Hitler was a clear case of necrophilia, and Hitler and Stalin with their unlimited capacity and willingness to kill and destroy were loved by the necrophiles.

Fromm goes on to say that the necrophile, by extension in modern society, might be labeled *homo mechanicus* who "has more pride in, and is more fascinated by, devices that can kill millions of people across several thousands of miles in minutes than he is depressed and frightened by the possibility of such mass destructon."

"If more people became aware of the difference between love of life and love of death," Fromm goes on to say, "if they became aware that they themselves are already far gone in the direction of indifference or necrophilia, the shock alone could produce new and healthy reactions. . . . Many might see through the pious rationalizations of the death lovers and change their admiration for them to disgust. Beyond this, our hypothesis would suggest one thing to those concerned with peace and survival: that every effort must be made to weaken the attraction of death, and to strengthen the attraction of life. Why not declare that there is only one truly dangerous subversion, the subversion of life?"

Why do not those who represent the traditions of religion and humanism speak up and say that there is no deadlier sin than love of death and contempt for life?*

These are the kinds of questions the young are asking—not only those who demonstrate and dissent but those, too, who go unwilling aboard the jet aircrafts that daily fly from the West Coast to Saigon. There are "bums" among them, of course, but on both sides—the bomb makers and the droppers of excreta in college deans' offices on one, and those who will turn their guns on frightened women and children or make as much money as they can in the black market on the other. But, by and large, the young of today are life-affirmers of a seemingly new breed who may at last, I think, give meaning to the worn phrases of generations of graduation speakers about their being "the hope of the future."

However, the task of strengthening the "attraction of life," the core of the American optimism that built this country, is in the hands of those no longer young. It is my generation who must halt, then turn back the incursions the military have made in our *civilian* system. These incursions have subverted or muffled civilian voices within the Executive branch, weakened the constitutional role and responsibility of the Congress, and laid an economic and psychological burden on the public that could be disastrous.

* "Creators and Destroyers," *Saturday Review,* January 4, 1964, pp. 22–25.

Index

Index

160

Index

162

Index

Index